Jill J. Dixon holds a B.S. in English Education and a Master's Degree in Special Education (summa cum laude). Her teaching experience spans twenty-one years of working with students in grades K-12, including physically handicapped, emotionally disturbed and learning disabled children. For four years she directed a prep school program which she founded for learning disabled and ADHD children and adolescents. Jill presently operates Educational Testing and Consulting Services and serves as a National Consultant for Home School Legal Defense Association, while home schooling three of her four children. She is the published author of several tests and educational materials.

Mrs. Dixon is available as a conference and workshop speaker on topics such as "ADHD: Fact or Fiction?", "The 5 R's of Homeschooling–What's Really Important?", "The Joy of Learning–Understanding Unique Learning Styles", "Creating Wonderful Writers", and "Assessing Our Children Effectively". Contact her at the address listed below.

DIAGNOSTIC PRESCRIPTIVE SERVICES
122 ROSE DHU WAY
SAVANNAH, GA 31419
www.edudps.com

WRITE WITH THE BEST – Vol. 2

Copyright © 2003 by Jill J. Dixon and T. L. Dixon

ALL RIGHTS RESERVED. No part of this publication may be reproduced or transmitted in any form or by any means, electronic or mechanical, including photocopy, recording, or by any information storage and retrieval system, without prior permission in writing from the publisher and the author.

Printed in U.S.A.

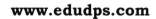

I dedicate this curriculum to my four children, who, by their presence, have always challenged me to do my best!

Special thanks to my oldest son, Evan, for his enthusiastic assistance with the literary passages.

www.edudps.com

TABLE OF CONTENTS

	PAGE
INTRODUCTION	6
HOW TO USE THIS PROGRAM	10
SPECIAL NOTES #1, #2, AND #3	13
UNIT 1: **WRITING POETRY – FREE VERSE** "The Railway Train" by Emily Dickinson	15
UNIT 2: **WRITING A BUSINESS LETTER –** To Sir John Everett Millais Perkins Institution for the Blind by Helen Keller	20
UNIT 3: **TAKING NOTES – WRITING OUTLINES – WRITING SUMMARIES –**	25
UNIT 4: **WRITING ESSAYS – PERSUASIVE AND EXPOSITORY** "Common Sense" by Thomas Paine "Of Studies" by Francis Bacon	29
UNIT 5: **WRITING A LITERARY CRITIQUE AND A BOOK REVIEW –** LITERARY CRITIQUE by Edgar Allan Poe of Nathaniel Hawthorne's *Twice-Told Tales*	43

Diagnostic Prescriptive Services

www.edudps.com

BOOK REVIEW by William Dean Howells
of Mark Twain's *The Adventures of Tom Sawyer*

UNIT 6:	WRITING A NEWSPAPER ARTICLE – "Would 'Treat 'Em Rough'" by Ernest Hemingway	57
UNIT 7:	WRITING A SPEECH – "In Defense of Rabirius – Before the Senate" by Marcus Tullius Cicero	64
UNIT 8:	WRITING A DRAMATIC MONOLOGUE – Mark Antony in *Julius Caesar* by William Shakespeare	72

LEARNING STYLES SUGGESTIONS — 78
AND OTHER WAYS TO AUGMENT THIS CURRICULUM

ADDITIONAL LITERARY PASSAGES — 80
FOR MODELING WRITING

HOW TO WRITE GUIDE — 83
    HOW TO WRITE A POEM IN FREE VERSE — 83
    HOW TO WRITE A BUSINESS LETTER — 85
    HOW TO TAKE NOTES — 87
    HOW TO WRITE AN OUTLINE — 87
    HOW TO WRITE A SUMMARY — 90
    HOW TO WRITE A PERSUASIVE ESSAY — 92

HOW TO WRITE AN EXPOSITORY ESSAY	**94**
HOW TO WRITE A LITERARY CRITIQUE AND A BOOK REVIEW	**96**
HOW TO WRITE A NEWSPAPER ARTICLE	**99**
HOW TO WRITE A SPEECH	**100**
HOW TO WRITE A DRAMATIC MONOLOGUE	**102**

GRADING CRITERIA — **103**

PROOFREADING CHECKLISTS FOR WRITING:

POETRY IN FREE VERSE	**104**
A BUSINESS LETTER	**105**
AN OUTLINE	**106**
A SUMMARY	**107**
PERSUASIVE ESSAYS	**108**
EXPOSITORY ESSAYS	**108**
A LITERARY CRITIQUE	**109**
A BOOK REVIEW	**110**
A NEWSPAPER ARTICLE	**111**
A SPEECH	**112**
A DRAMATIC MONOLOGUE	**113**
GENERAL PURPOSE PROOFREADING CHECKLIST	**114**

SELECT ANSWER KEY TO CITED LITERARY PASSAGES — **115**

SELECT LITERARY PASSAGES — **125**

INTRODUCTION

Except for two words, the <u>first</u> <u>two</u> paragraphs that follow are restated verbatim from Volume 1.

It doesn't take long, when looking in educational arenas – homeschool, public, and private – to discover that writing has been one of the most neglected subjects of our modern educational era. In the state in which I live, mandatory educational reforms have been made to improve the writing skills of students in elementary, middle, and high-school grades. This was finally accomplished because state colleges complained about incoming freshman who were unable to write even a paragraph adequately. The large majority of these students were required to take remedial composition classes before they could enter regular freshman English classes. In twelve to thirteen years of public or private education, they were never taught to write. Unfortunately, I have also seen this trend among homeschooled children. In the writing classes that I teach, I have found that many students have been taught to write sentences and brief paragraphs, but have never moved beyond that point into proficiency in various writing genres. For example, they have no idea how to correctly write a letter, compose poetry or write an essay and have no idea what it means to write descriptively. We all know that competent writing is essential in our age of communication and is a huge component of an excellent <u>and</u> complete education.

This curriculum was devised as a result of twenty-one years of teaching writing to students in grades K-5 through 12, including public, private, and homeschooled children. Many of the ideas presented in this book were used in a homeschool writing class that I have taught for the last five years. I used classical literature and other great works as models of excellent writing, while teaching students literary appreciation and analysis at the same time. Students were required to bring in weekly samples of "excellent" writing and to be able to explain what made the writing "excellent". They took weekly dictation from the passages and modeled their assignments after these writings. Amazing improvements were made, and many of my students who had been diagnosed as having learning disabilities in written expression began to enjoy writing for the first time in their lives. I also interviewed homeschooling parents who were dissatisfied with the writing curriculums they had used thus far, and I found that they desired a curriculum that taught writing systematically, yet in a simple and clear way. They requested that a guide be included in the curriculum that would provide instructions on exactly how to write specific genres. Many parents also indicated that their students became bored with various curriculums because they did not offer interesting activities, etc. All of these issues have been addressed in this program. In addition to the instructions contained within the curriculum, a helpful "HOW TO WRITE GUIDE" is included to assist parents in the teaching of each genre. A chapter entitled "Additional Literary Passages For Modeling Writing" is also included. Both of these make it possible for parents to continue teaching writing by using my approach, even after the initial literary passages are used. The greatest way for students to learn to write is through continued practice, so I have included resources to insure the continuation of writing skills. <u>Proofreading</u> and <u>listening comprehension</u> skills, which are essential to successful writing, <u>are also taught</u>, and all learning styles are accommodated.

The curriculum contains excerpts from great works of world literature and writings by great authors of world literature. Although all genres for excellent writing are listed in the complete set, each volume stands alone as complete regarding the genres that it contains. Volume 1 naturally begins with the prerequisites of successful writing and progresses until the end of volume 2. Volume 1 is for grades 3-12 and Volume 2 is for grades 6-12. You are not required to purchase separate books for each grade level. Devised in this way, the curriculum is also very cost effective.

There are two main reasons why *WRITE WITH THE BEST* contains several different genres of writing.

First, it is a known fact that students learn to become good writers by writing, writing, and writing. The more genres they are exposed to, the more writing experience they will gain.

Secondly, to be proficient writers, students must learn to write a variety of genres and not just know how to write a paragraph or book report. The more kinds of writing they are proficient in, the more equipped they will be to "write with the best"!

§
Focus and Goal

The focus and goal of this writing program are effective and simple. Its purpose is to zero in on the skills that produce excellent writing and to teach students to use these same skills. To accomplish this, the program doesn't abstractly emphasize various grammatical rules for composition, but rather focuses on the *actual skills* of successful, excellent writers and teaches the observation and emulation of these same skills. Grammar is taught in the context of writing, not as a separate subject. The effective method of this curriculum follows in the *literary* steps of writers of great works of world literature, modeling writing after their methods and techniques for successful composition. *In summary, the focus of this program is to teach students to write* **descriptively, persuasively, and informatively** *through emulating the actual skills of masters of great writing. The goal of this program is to produce successful writers who know how to write effectively, who know how to proofread their work efficiently, and who know how to properly analyze great writing.*

www.edudps.com

HOW TO USE THIS PROGRAM

1. *WRITE WITH THE BEST, Vol. 2* was designed to be used for a total of 20 weeks, making it possible to complete the curriculum twice each year. Many parents, however, will want to extend each unit to insure mastery of the material and use the program for a full year. Students who have never written an essay or a speech before may need more than the allotted time to perfect each skill. It is *very important* that students master each prerequisite skill before moving on, even if this takes a great deal of time. The objective is mastery of each writing genre. I personally recommend going through the curriculum slowly once a year.

2. I highly encourage teachers to have their students write about topics that they are studying in other areas, such as history or science. It is a proven fact that children retain information much better if it is incorporated into as many subjects as possible. An example of this would be to write a business letter to George Washington while you are studying the American Revolution or to write an expository essay about the cottage industry while you are studying the Industrial Revolution.

3. Evaluate the writing of your students according to their ages and ability levels. For example, if you have two students (one in 6th grade and one in 12th), you certainly cannot expect the same quality of writing from both students. A simple dramatic monologue with 5-6 sentences will suffice for a sixth grader, but an older student would be expected to write a longer and more detailed dramatic monologue. However, keep in mind that this does not include students with learning difficulties. Also, regardless of age or grade level, if a student has not learned the elementary skills of writing, evaluate him as a beginner.

4. Each family must have a dictionary and a thesaurus. I suggest *Webster's New Collegiate Dictionary,* current edition. An English handbook may also be beneficial for parents. Many parents will want to provide additional practice in capitalization, punctuation, English usage and using specific parts of speech. Many excellent English workbooks cover these skills. For students in grades 6-8, I recommend *Daily Grams* and *Easy Grammar.* For students in grades 8 and up, I recommend reading Strunk and White's *The Elements of Style* once each year before beginning this writing program. I also recommend that each student (grades 8 and up) complete a research paper on a chosen or given topic each year, preferably in the last 2 months of the school year. I have not included this skill in this volume because there are several excellent guides available that teach how to write an effective research paper. Students need to learn these research skills as early as possible to become proficient in this skill before possible college admission.

5. To thoroughly utilize the "Proofreading Checklist", some students will need instruction in some of the skills addressed in the checklist such as run-on sentences and subject-verb agreement. Any English handbook will cover these, as will most English workbooks. For additional practice with proofreading skills, I recommend *Editor-In-Chief* or *Great Editing Adventures*. However, the best practice for proofreading skills is for students to constantly proofread their own papers, which is an effective feature of WRITE WITH THE BEST.

6. Some students may have difficulty reading the literary passages by themselves. If this is the case, parents should read these to the students while the students follow along. For students who have motor difficulties or problems writing down their thoughts on paper, it is totally acceptable for teachers to write what their students dictate to them. This can be done with each objective that requires writing on

the part of the student.

7. The teacher should read the objectives of all the days of each unit before the student begins so that the progression of the curriculum can be realized. There is a calculated progression in the program. Also, some days are extended into the following days.

8. Teachers must make sure that <u>all</u> of the objectives of each day are achieved so that the goal of this curriculum, mastery of good writing skills, can be realized.

9. Emphasis in the form of **bold** text, *italicized* text, <u>underscored</u> text, and "quotation marks" is used throughout the book. Each different kind of emphasis is utilized for clarification of each objective so that the student will not miss <u>each important</u> element within each objective. Sometimes emphasis is not repeated when the objectives restate issues.

10. Students should look up the definitions of all unfamiliar words in the literary passages while reading or listening to the passages. This will help improve their vocabulary and comprehension skills. Writings of great authors are excellent for teaching vocabulary. If your student finds any of the passages difficult to understand, realize these passages were chosen to teach vocabulary <u>and</u> writing skills.

11. Parents are permitted to copy only the pages containing the cited literary passages and the actual proofreading checklists for their students' use. You will need to make copies of the pages containing the cited literary passages and the proofreading checklists if you are using the book for more than one student or if you desire to maintain the book unmarked. Therefore, under such circumstances, making copies of these passages and the proofreading checklists is not just permitted, but also recommended.

12. A select answer key has been provided in the back of this book to verify the student's work. Regarding parts of speech, <u>only descriptive</u> adjectives, verbs, adverbs, and <u>specific</u> nouns are listed. <u>Not all</u>

nouns, verbs, adjectives, and adverbs are included. The verbs, adjectives, and adverbs listed are color specified in order to facilitate use of the answer key.

§

Special Note #1 (with additions to that of Vol. 1)

We have chosen the great authors and works of world literature found in this program because of their incomparable **themes, characters, techniques, persuasion, descriptions, and styles of writing.** Even though these authors were excellent writers, some times they did <u>not</u> follow a number of our modern rules for punctuation and sentence structure or utilize our modern <u>models</u> for writing. Therefore, we have corrected some of the punctuation and sentence structure in the literary passages, but have not changed any of the essential structure of the passages. Furthermore, when teaching your students, please point out to them that we are modeling these writers because of their content, style, superb descriptive skills, and persuasive techniques. When they depart from our modern rules of punctuation, structure, and our models for writing, we will follow the proper requirements as stated in the "HOW TO WRITE GUIDE" and your English handbook or workbook. **In summary, our aim is to combine the best of both worlds – superlative writing style and correct writing form.**

Special Note #2

We have not changed the spelling in the various literary passages cited. We have reproduced the spelling as rendered by each author.

Special Note #3

Using the analogy of a journey up a mountain, the skills learned in Volume 1 can be likened to the beginning of the trek. In that volume, we mainly focused on *descriptive* writing skills as we learned to master its genres. In this volume, as previously indicated, we will mainly focus on *informative*, *persuasive*, and *procedural* writing skills as we learn to master these genres. In taking this approach, we will progress to the top of the mountain. Accordingly, the method of this volume will employ a greater refinement in its execution than Volume 1 did. For example, within the units of Volume 1, the student was instructed to use the "HOW TO WRITE GUIDE" on a limited basis. In this volume the student will utilize the "HOW TO WRITE GUIDE" on a regular basis as essential to the completeness of each unit. Moreover, because of the *nature* and *similar aspects* of the genres covered, in this volume I have employed a greater degree of repetition, essential for learning to master these particular genres. I have, nonetheless, endeavored to keep the method of this volume within the same simple and effective scope as that of the previous volume. Be sure to remind your students to utilize the skills learned in Volume 1 of this curriculum in the daily objectives of this volume when it's appropriate. Although I will touch on those skills throughout this volume, it is largely left to each student to use the descriptive writing skills that they were taught in Volume 1 as they learn to master the genres of Volume 2. Our goal is to reach the summit of writing, invigorated and able, not tired and ineffective.

UNIT 1
WRITING POETRY
- FREE VERSE -

Day 1 7 Objectives (each objective is indicated by an asterisk)

*Read the poem "The Railway Train" by Emily Dickinson. Another title for this poem is "I Like to See It Lap the Miles".

THE RAILWAY TRAIN

I like to see it lap the miles,
And lick the valleys up,
And stop to feed itself at tanks;
And then, prodigious, step

Around a pile of mountains,
And, supercilious, peer
In shanties by the sides of roads;
And then a quarry pare

To fit its sides, and crawl between,
Complaining all the while
In horrid, hooting stanza;
Then chase itself down hill

And neigh like Boanerges;
Then, punctual as a star,

> Stop -- docile and omnipotent --
> At its own stable door.

*Look up all unfamiliar words in the dictionary such as "prodigious" and "supercilious". The use of "Boanerges" is called an allusion.

⇒ **Allusion:** a reference to a familiar person, thing, event, or place in a literary passage to *enhance* the theme or make a *comparison*.

*If you haven't done so already, look up "Boanerges" and write down its meaning. Why do you think that Ms. Dickinson used it here? *Read the poem again now that you understand the meanings of the words. *Now close your eyes and have someone read it to you out loud. What images did you see *immediately*? *Name all of the things that the train is compared to. *Does this poem rhyme?

Day 2   3 Objectives

*Consider the definitions of *specific* **nouns**, *descriptive* **verbs**, and *descriptive* **adjectives**. (If you need to, review these definitions from Vol. 1 of WRITE WITH THE BEST.) *Read the poem from yesterday again. *Circle all *specific* **nouns**. Underline all *descriptive* **verbs** in green and all *descriptive* **adjectives** in red. (See the Answer Key to verify the student's work.)

Day 3   3 Objectives

Memorize the following definitions and *discuss* them with your teacher.

   Poetry: language that shows imagination, deep emotion and/or thinking in verse form

   Free verse: poetry that does not have a regular meter or rhyme scheme

Figure of Speech: a form of expression used to create a special feeling or convey meaning by making an interesting or creative comparison (For example: metaphor, simile, personification, or hyperbole)

Imagery: the actual words that a poet uses to bring forth images or pictures in the mind of the reader

Simile: the comparison of two unlike objects using the words "like" or "as" – Example: "My love is *like* a red, red rose."

Personification: a figure of speech in which an animal, object, or idea takes on characteristics of a person – Example: "The rain *danced* on the street."

Alliteration: the repetition of initial consonant sounds in two or more words of a line or phrase of poetry, used to appeal to the ear – Example: "**B**ooth led **b**oldly with his **b**ig **b**ass drum."

Tone: the author's outlook or attitude toward his subject and the devices that he uses to create the mood of his literary work

Rhythm: the repetition of beat or the measured flow of words in poetry

*Write two of *your own* examples of (a) simile (b) personification and (c) alliteration.

Day 4   3 Objectives

*Review *all* definitions from yesterday.
*Write down the answers to these questions about Ms. Dickinson's poem:
  1. What *animal characteristics* does the poet give to the train in the first stanza?
  2. What *human characteristics* are given in the third stanza?
  3. In the last stanza, what are the two *similes*?
  4. In the third stanza, what is the example of *alliteration*?

5. Even though this poem does not rhyme, does it have *rhythm*?
6. What interesting detail does the author end the poem with?
7. What is the *tone* of this poem?
8. What animal does Ms. Dickinson emphasize through the imagery of her poem?

*Write in your own words what you think that Ms. Dickinson is saying in this poem.

Day 5   5 Objectives

*Find another poem in *free verse* by a well-known author in a book that you have at home or from the library. *List all of the *images* or *pictures* that this poem portrays. *List all *figures of speech* in the poem. *Look for *allusions* in this poem. If you find any, write these down. *Compare this poem to "The Railway Train", looking for the same kinds of *features* dealt with in the questions from yesterday.

Day 6   4 Objectives

Today you will prepare to write your own poem in free verse.
*Read "HOW TO WRITE A POEM IN FREE VERSE" on pages 83-84. *Choose the subject of your poem. Make sure that you choose something that you can adequately describe. *Decide on your *theme* or the *message* that you will convey through your poem. *Decide on the *tone* of your poem. For example, is it serious, lighthearted, or sad?

Day 7   3 Objectives

*Write down *descriptive* words and phrases that come to mind when you think of your *subject, theme,* and *tone.* Also, come up with some *figures of speech and some *sound devices to use such as alliteration. <u>Do</u> <u>not</u> use too much alliteration. Remember Ms. Dickinson's singular and effective use of alliteration.

Day 8   2 Objectives

*Start writing your poem by jotting down your initial ideas, and keep writing until *every line* says exactly what you want it to say. *<u>Make</u> <u>sure</u> that you are creating *pictures* in your readers' minds through the use of *specific* **nouns** and *vivid* or descriptive **adjectives**, **verbs**, and **adverbs**.

Day 9   3 Objectives

*End your poem today with something *exciting* or an *interesting detail*. *Read your poem out loud to make sure that you have included <u>all</u> necessary details discussed on Day 3. How does your poem's details compare to Ms. Dickinson's? *Proofread your poem thoroughly, using the proofreading checklists on pages 104 and 114.

Day 10   2 Objectives

*Rewrite or type your poem. You may also want to illustrate your poem with a drawing or painting. *Keep your completed poem in a folder to serve as your writing portfolio.

www.edudps.com

UNIT 2
WRITING A BUSINESS LETTER

Background: Miss Helen Keller was eleven years old when she wrote both letters that appear in this volume. Because of her age, parts of her letters appear to be more like friendly letters than business letters. However, they <u>are</u> business letters.

Day 1 4 Objectives (each objective is indicated by an asterisk)

*Read the following business letter by Helen Keller.

April 30, 1891

Sir John Everett Millais
Perkins Institution for the Blind
South Boston, Mass.

My Dear Mr. Millais:

Your little American sister is going to write you a letter because she wants you to know how pleased she was to hear you were interested in our poor little Tommy and had sent some money to help educate him. It is very beautiful to think that people far away in England feel sorry for a little helpless child in America. I used to think, when I read in my books about your great city, that when I visited it the people would be strangers to me, but now I feel differently. It seems to me that all people who have loving, pitying hearts are not strangers to each other. I can hardly wait patiently for the time to come when I shall see my dear English friends and their beautiful island home. My favourite poet has written some lines about England which I love very much. I think you will like them too, so I will try to write them for you.

"Hugged in the clinging billow's clasp,
From seaweed fringe to mountain heather,
The British oak with rooted grasp
Her slender handful holds together,
With cliffs of white and bowers of green,
And ocean narrowing to caress her,
And hills and threaded streams between,
Our little mother isle, God bless her!"

You will be glad to hear that Tommy has a kind lady to teach him and that he is a pretty active little fellow. He loves to climb much better than to spell, but that is because he does not know yet what a wonderful thing language is. He cannot imagine how very, very happy he will be when he can tell us his thoughts, and we can tell him how we have loved him so long.

Tomorrow April will hide her tears and blushes beneath the flowers of lovely May. I wonder if the May-days in England are as beautiful as they are here. Now I must say good-bye. Please think of me always.

Your loving little sister,
HELEN KELLER

*Write down the *purpose* of Miss Keller's letter in your own words. *Write down what impressed you *the most* about the way that she expressed herself. *Tell all the ways Miss Keller made the letter interesting for her reader.

Day 2 6 Objectives

*Read "HOW TO WRITE A BUSINESS LETTER" on page 85. *Read Miss Helen Keller's letter again. Does she include a *beginning, middle,* and *concluding* paragraph? *Mark them each as #1, #2, and #3 respectively. *Underline the *stated purpose* of the letter. Remember that because of Miss Keller's age, her letter resembles a friendly letter in places. *Make a copy of her letter and using the rules that you learned from "HOW TO WRITE A BUSINESS LETTER", correct her letter in each place where those rules should apply. *Place her corrected letter in your writing portfolio.

Day 3 1 Objective

*Pick someone to write a business letter to. Think of someone that you would like to request information from, lodge a complaint with, or thank or ask for a service. For example, you may have a politician that you want to ask to consider a specific law or bill.

Day 4   3 Objectives

*Find another business letter around your house or in a book. Ask your parents for a copy of a business letter that they have written or received. *Is this letter written in the correct form? (Compare it to the form on page 86.) Does it have all the parts that a business letter should have? (Compare it to the points on page 85.) *Is the *purpose* of this letter clear?

Day 5   2 Objectives

*Write down your *specific purpose* for writing your business letter. *List specific and interesting things that you want to say or ask.

Day 6   4 Objectives

*Read "HOW TO WRITE A BUSINESS LETTER" again, paying special attention to facts about writing the introduction.
You will write your introductory paragraph today. *Introduce yourself and *state the purpose* of your letter. *Make sure that your purpose is *clear*.

Day 7   4 Objectives

*Write your *body* paragraph. Remember that this paragraph is where you will present your information or thoroughly explain your purpose for writing. Make sure that this main paragraph *begins* with a topic sentence and *ends* with a concluding sentence. *Also include your interesting facts or information here.

Day 8 1 Objective

*Write your *concluding* paragraph by following the rules for a concluding paragraph on page 85.

Day 9 4 Objectives

*Read Miss Keller's letter again, taking note of her *purpose* and *tone*.
*Read your letter out loud to yourself or someone else. *<u>Make</u> <u>sure</u> the *purpose* of your letter is *clear* and that it is written in a *polite* and *respectful* tone. *Proofread your letter using the checklists on pages 105 and 114.

Day 10 2 Objectives

*If possible, type the final copy of your letter. If you are unable to type it, then neatly write it in cursive or print it. *Place it in your portfolio or mail it, only under the supervision of your parents. If you mail it, first make a copy for your portfolio.

www.edudps.com

UNIT 3

TAKING NOTES - WRITING OUTLINES - WRITING SUMMARIES

Please Note: This unit does not include any great authors of world literature used as writing models because there are none available. However, the skills of learning how to take notes, how to write an outline and how to write a summary are essential, not only for general educational purposes, but also for essay and speech writing and other genres covered in this volume.

Day 1 3 Objectives (each objective is indicated by an asterisk)

*With the help of your teacher, pick a newspaper or magazine article. Try to find something that you are interested in or would like to learn about. The article must be factual, *not* fictional. (You will be using this article to learn how to take notes and write an outline and a summary.) *Skim the article to gain general understanding and meaning. What do you think that the writer is trying to say? *Write this down.

Day 2 5 Objectives

Today you will learn how to take notes.
⇒ Note taking is realized in a few simple steps. To fully grasp this skill, you will need *repeated* practice. Starting now, learn to take notes *daily* from your school reading assignments, etc.
*Using the same article from yesterday, read it *carefully*. ***Highlight** or underline any *key words* or *phrases* as you read. Keep in mind that usually the first and last lines of paragraphs are summary statements and contain main points or ideas. *Read the article a second time and look for the *main ideas* and *necessary details* of the selection. *Write down

these main points or ideas. Do not write down everything but just the *most important* points. *Write these down in concise form. A good note taker remembers to be concise.

Please note: There is no proofreading checklist for taking notes.

Day 3 2 Objectives

Today and tomorrow you will learn how to write an outline.
*Read "HOW TO WRITE AN OUTLINE" on pages 87-90 in the "HOW TO WRITE GUIDE". *Decide whether you want to write a *topical* or *sentence* outline about the article that you worked on during Days 1 and 2.

Day 4 1 Objective

Follow carefully the directions for writing an outline on pages 87-90, and using your notes that you took on Day 2, write an outline of your newspaper or magazine article. Make sure that you follow the outline form carefully. (See again the sample outlines on pages 89-90.)

Day 5 3 Objectives

*Read your article again, and *make sure that your outline has covered all of the main points. *Proofread your outline by using the proofreading checklist on page 106.

Day 6 3 Objectives

For the next five days, you will learn how to write effective summaries. Once again, you will be using your newspaper or magazine article that you picked on Day 1 of this unit.

*Read "HOW TO WRITE A SUMMARY" on pages 90-91. *Decide on a topic sentence for your summary. *Remember* that the topic sentence will tell *what* your summary will be about. Your topic sentence must say something about the main idea of your article or basically what the writer of your article was trying to say. *Write this topic sentence down.

Day 7   5 Objectives

*Begin to write your summary by using the main ideas that you wrote down on Day 2 of this unit. *Refer to your outline that you wrote on Day 4. *Start with your topic sentence from yesterday and *write this summary in your own words. You cannot add any new ideas, but must simply restate the ideas from the article that you read. You should include any important names, dates, places and times from the article. *Remember to never say in a summary, "This article was about...." Write *just like* the author of the article did, but *in your own words.*

Day 8   3 Objectives

*Write the concluding sentence for your paragraph summary. This sentence is a restatement (in different words) of your topic sentence. *Read your completed summary out loud, and *make sure that you have followed all of the guidelines in the "HOW TO WRITE GUIDE" on "HOW TO WRITE A SUMMARY":

    Have you written only the *main points* of the article?

    Have you written the summary *in your own words,* but not added your *own ideas?*

    Have you made clear the author's purpose for writing the article?

Day 9   1 Objective

*Proofread your article using the proofreading checklist on pages 107 and 114.

Day 10   2 Objectives

*Rewrite or type your summary. Staple your article or a copy of it to the summary, and *place them in your portfolio.

UNIT 4
WRITING ESSAYS

Please Note: This unit is four weeks long.

PART 1 – WRITING PERSUASIVE ESSAYS

⇒ **Persuasive essay:** a composition of related paragraphs in which the author tries to <u>convince</u> the readers <u>to</u> <u>believe</u> his viewpoint.

Background: The persuasive essay that I have chosen is an excerpt from "Common Sense" by Thomas Paine. It was written in January 1776, six months before the "Declaration of Independence" was finalized.

Day 1 5 Objectives (each objective is indicated by an asterisk)

*Memorize the definition of a persuasive assay given above.
*Do brief research into the life of Thomas Paine to discover <u>why</u> he wrote this essay. To understand his motive and purpose in writing "Common Sense" is to understand the foundations of this persuasive essay.
*Read the following excerpt from the essay "Common Sense". *As you read, write down the definitions of any unfamiliar words to enable you to better understand what Mr. Paine is saying.

COMMON SENSE

Thoughts on the Present State of American Affairs

I challenge the warmest advocate for reconciliation, to shew, a single advantage that this continent can reap, by being connected with Great Britain. I repeat the challenge, not a single advantage is derived. Our corn will fetch its price in any market in Europe, and our imported goods must be paid for, buy them where we will. But the injuries and disadvantages we sustain by that connection, are without number; and our duty to mankind at large, as well as to ourselves, instruct us to renounce the alliance.

Any submission to, or dependence on Great Britain, tends directly to involve this continent in European wars and quarrels; and sets us at variance with nations, who would otherwise seek our friendship, and against whom, we have neither anger nor complaint. As Europe is our market for trade, we ought to form no partial connection with any part of it. It is the true interest of America to steer clear of European contentions, which she never can do, while by her dependence on Britain, she is made the make-weight in the scale of British politics.

Europe is too thickly planted with kingdoms to be long at peace, and whenever a war breaks out between England and any foreign power, the trade of America goes to ruin, BECAUSE OF HER CONNECTION WITH ENGLAND. The next war may not turn out like the last, and should it not, the advocates for reconciliation now, will be wishing for separation then, because, neutrality in that case, would be a safer convoy than a man of war. Every thing that is right or natural pleads for separation. The blood of the slain, the weeping voice of nature cries, 'TIS TIME TO PART.

Even the distance at which the Almighty hath placed England and America, is a strong and natural proof, that the authority of the one, over the other, was never the design of Heaven. The time likewise at which the continent was discovered, adds weight to the argument, and the manner in which it was peopled increases the force of it. The reformation was preceded by the discovery of America, as if the Almighty graciously meant to open a sanctuary to the Persecuted in future years, when home should afford neither friendship nor safety.

The authority of Great Britain over this continent, is a form of government, which sooner or later must have an end: and a serious mind can draw no true pleasure by looking forward under the painful and positive conviction, that what he calls "the present constitution" is merely temporary. As parents, we can have no joy, knowing that THIS GOVERNMENT is not sufficiently lasting to ensure any thing which we may bequeath to posterity: and by a plain method of argument, as we are running the next generation into debt, we ought to do the work of it, otherwise we use them meanly and pitifully. In order to discover the line of our duty rightly, we should take our children in our hand, and fix our station a few years farther into life; that eminence will present a prospect, which a few present fears and prejudices conceal from our sight.

Men of passive tempers look somewhat lightly over the offenses of Britain, and, still hoping for the best, are apt to call out, "COME, COME, WE SHALL BE FRIENDS AGAIN, FOR

ALL THIS." But examine the passions and feelings of mankind, bring the doctrine of reconciliation to the touchstone of nature, and then tell me, whether you can hereafter love, honor, and faithfully serve the power that hath carried fire and sword into your land? If you cannot do all these, then are you only deceiving yourselves, and by your delay bringing ruin upon posterity. Your future connection with Britain, whom you can neither love nor honor will be forced and unnatural, and being formed only on the plan of present convenience, will in a little time fall into a relapse more wretched than the first. But if you say, you can still pass the violations over, then I ask, hath your house been burnt? Hath your property been destroyed before your face! Are your wife and children destitute of a bed to lie on, or bread to live on? Have you lost a parent or a child by their hands, and yourself the ruined and wretched survivor! If you have not, then are you not a judge of those who have. But if you have, and still can shake hands with the murderers, then are you unworthy the name of husband, father, friend, or lover, and whatever may be your rank or title in life, you have the heart of a coward, and the spirit of a sycophant.

O, ye that love mankind! Ye that dare oppose not only the tyranny but the tyrant, stand forth! Every spot of the old world is overrun with opposition. Freedom hath been hunted round the globe. Asia and Africa have long expelled her. Europe regards her like a stranger, and England hath given her warning to depart. O receive the fugitive, and prepare in time an asylum for mankind.

*From your first reading, what do you think that Mr. Paine is saying?

Day 2   7 Objectives

*Memorize the following definition of an essay.
⇒ **Essay:** a composition of related paragraphs where ideas on a specific topic are described, explained, and/or argued for in an interesting way.

*What is distinctive about a *persuasive* essay?
  ➢ While it's important that you learn how to master all of the writing genres covered in volumes 1 and 2, it is <u>very important</u> that you learn to write effective essays because essay writing will be a *significant* part of your education for several years and your *chief* form of writing and test taking if you attend college. Essay writing is also a <u>very important</u> skill necessary for *effective communication* in everyday life.

*Memorize the following definition of a thesis statement.
⇒ **Thesis statement:** a statement that identifies the main focus and purpose of a written work. (In a persuasive essay, this statement must be an arguable statement – one that can be *realistically* argued, having at least two sides.)

*Read #6 only in "HOW TO WRITE A PERSUASIVE ESSAY" on page 93.

Please note: Not all earlier writers followed the same "rules" of writing that we follow today such as making the thesis statement the last sentence in the introductory paragraph.

*Read the first paragraph from "Common Sense". What is Mr. Paine's thesis statement in this paragraph? *<u>Underline</u> his thesis statement.

How does Mr. Paine grab the attention of his readers in the first paragraph? *Write this down.

Day 3   6 Objectives

⇒ All other paragraphs after the introductory paragraph are called supporting paragraphs, except for the very last paragraph in the essay which is the concluding paragraph.

*Read the entire excerpt from Mr. Paine's essay again.
*Consider Mr. Paine's supporting paragraphs. What are his arguments to support his thesis statement? *Underline these arguments. *Write down the main points. *Examine Mr. Paine's concluding paragraph. How does he leave his readers with a lasting, final thought? *Write this down.

Day 4   6 Objectives

*Read "HOW TO WRITE A PERSUASIVE ESSAY" on pages 92-93.
*Come up with a topic for a persuasive essay. Your teacher may choose to give you a topic relating to something that you are studying in literature or history. Remember that this topic must be debatable; in other words, it must be an opinion that can be truly argued and has at least two sides. See "HOW TO WRITE A PERSUASIVE ESSAY" on page 92 again for ideas on different types of persuasive essays. *Decide which type you will write. *Narrow your topic down so that you can specifically and effectively argue your point. *Write your thesis statement. Spend some time working on this statement. It is really the most important part of your essay. *Make sure that your thesis statement is clear to your readers.

Day 5 5 Objectives

*Write down everything that you know about your topic. *<u>Make</u> <u>sure</u> that you have enough *facts* and *details* to <u>support</u> your argument or thesis statement – facts that can bolster your argument in a factual debate. *To prove a point, use statistics, quotes, etc. Do research, if necessary, in order to accomplish these objectives. *Organize all of your information in a sentence or topical outline. *Write your thesis statement at the top of your outline.

Day 6 5 Objectives

*Begin writing your essay today. <u>Never</u> say, "I am going to write about...." or "This essay is about...." in your introductory paragraph. *Come up with an "attention grabber" that you will use to gain the attention of your readers <u>right</u> <u>up</u> <u>front</u>. See #6 on page 93 for ideas for attention grabbers. *Put your attention grabber at the beginning of your introductory paragraph. *Write several sentences next in order to introduce your topic, and *then write your thesis statement as the <u>last</u> sentence in your introductory paragraph. **Note:** In essays, attention grabbers generally come <u>before</u> you introduce your topic.

Day 7 5 Objectives

*Decide on transition words that you will use to help your body paragraphs link together and give flow to your essay. Use words such as "first", "next", and "last". *Write your body paragraphs with <u>one</u> paragraph for *each argument* that you have listed in your outline. *<u>Make</u> <u>sure</u> the each paragraph has a <u>clear</u> topic sentence – a sentence that comes at the beginning of the paragraph and tells what the whole paragraph will be about. *<u>Make</u> <u>sure</u> that each paragraph <u>sticks</u> to your topic sentence and gives <u>specific</u> *examples*, *facts*, or *quotations* to support your argument. If you are writing about a topic from a piece of literature that you are reading, make sure that you use the literature to support your argument. Also, *<u>make</u> <u>sure</u> that each paragraph ends with a concluding sentence – one that restates the topic sentence.

Day 8   3 Objectives

*Begin to write your concluding paragraph by <u>restating</u> your thesis statement *in different words*. *Next, *summarize* the **main points** of your paper. *End your concluding paragraph with an "attention grabber" that leaves a <u>final</u> *gripping* or *lasting* thought in the minds of your readers. You can refer to the same list of attention grabbers used in the introductory paragraph, or you can use a *striking example* of your main argument. Look at Mr. Paine again for concluding ideas. His concluding paragraph was striking. Remember, <u>do</u> <u>not</u> introduce *new* ideas in your concluding paragraph.

Day 9   3 Objectives

*Read your entire essay out loud to make sure that you have truly argued your point effectively. *Proofread what you have written by using the proofreading checklists on pages 108 and 114. *<u>Make</u> <u>sure</u> that you have included <u>all</u> components for an effective essay.

Day 10   3 Objectives

*Rewrite or type your essay. *Read it to someone. *Place it in your writing portfolio.

UNIT 4 (CONTINUED)
WRITING ESSAYS

PART 2 – WRITING EXPOSITORY ESSAYS

⇒ **Expository essay:** a composition of related paragraphs that *informs* the reader about a meaningful subject.

Day 11   5 Objectives

*Memorize the definition of an expository essay given above.
*Read the following expository essay by Francis Bacon. *Write down the definitions of any unfamiliar words *as you read.* *Also, because Bacon is sometimes difficult to understand, use your note taking skills learned in Unit 3 *as you read.* (Use this same technique with other essay writers who can be difficult to understand.)

OF STUDIES

Studies serve for delight, for ornament, and for ability. Their chief use for delight is in privateness and retiring; for ornament is in discourse; and for ability is in the judgment and disposition of business. For expert men can execute and perhaps judge of particulars one by one, but the general counsels and the plots and marshalling of affairs come best from those that are learned.

To spend too much time in studies is sloth; to use them too much for ornament is affectation; to make judgment wholly by their rules is the humor of a scholar. They perfect nature and are perfected by experience: for natural abilities are like natural plants that need proyning by study; and studies themselves do give forth directions too much at large, except they be bounded in by experience. Crafty men contemn studies, simple men admire them, and wise men use them; for they teach not their own use, but that is a wisdom without them, and above them, won by observation.

Read not to contradict and confute; nor to believe and take for granted; nor to find talk and discourse; but to weigh and consider. Some books are to be tasted, others to be swallowed, and some few to be chewed and digested; that is, some books are to be read only in parts, others to be read, but not curiously, and some few to be read wholly, and with diligence and attention. Some books also may be read by deputy, and extracts made of them by others, but that would be only in the less important arguments, and the meaner sort of books. Distilled books are like common, distilled waters. They are flashy things. Reading maketh a full man; conference a ready man; and writing an exact man. And therefore, if a man write little, he had need have a great memory; if he confer little, he had need have a present wit; and if he read little, he had need have much cunning, to seem to know, what he doth not.

Histories make men wise; poets witty; the mathematics subtile; natural philosophy deep; morals grave; logic and rhetoric able to contend. Nay, there is no stond or impediment in the wit, but may be wrought out by fit studies. Like diseases of the body, these too have appropriate exercises. Bowling is good for the stone and reins; shooting for the lungs and breast; gentle walking for the stomach; riding for the head; and the like. So if a man's wit be wandering, let him study the mathematics; for in demonstrations, if his wit be called away never so little, he must begin again. If his wit be not apt to distinguish or find differences, or if he be not apt to beat over matters, let him study the schoolmen. To call up one thing to prove and illustrate another, let him study the lawyers' cases. So every defect of the mind, may have a special receipt.

*From your first reading, what do you think that the author is saying? What is he informing the reader about?

Day 12 6 Objectives

*Review the definition of an essay from Day 2 of this unit. *What is distinctive about an *expository* essay? *Review the definition of a thesis statement from Day 2 of this unit. *Reread Mr. Bacon's essay. *Underline the thesis statement of this expository essay. *Write down the answers to the following questions: *What* is this author explaining? In his explanation, is he *describing, comparing, presenting a problem,* or *telling how* to do something?

Day 13   2 Objectives

*To help you understand Mr. Bacon's essay *and* to develop your skill in writing outlines, write a topical outline of the essay. See Unit 3 and the "HOW TO WRITE GUIDE" for a refresher on topical outlines. Before you write your outline, *examine the expository essay for specific *examples* and *details*. Pay attention to Mr. Bacon's *thoroughness* in explaining his subject. Pay attention again to the *way* that he explained his subject. This will help you learn to emulate his skill.

Day 14   6 Objectives

*Read "HOW TO WRITE AN EXPOSITORY ESSAY" on pages 94-95. *Choose a topic that you would like to *explain* in an expository essay. Your teacher may want to give you a topic relating to something that you are presently studying. *Write down everything that you know about the topic that you have chosen. Your purpose is to *adequately* inform your readers, and you must have enough information and facts to do this. Do more research on your topic if you need to. *Narrow* your topic down, and *decide what the *focus* of your essay will be. See "HOW TO WRITE AN EXPOSITORY ESSAY" on page 94 again for different types of expository essays. *Decide which type you will write.

Day 15   2 Objectives

*Looking back at the information that you gathered yesterday, write your thesis statement. Your thesis statement must express a *specific feeling* or take a *specific stand* about the subject, but it cannot be a truly arguable or debatable opinion. *Write a sentence or topical outline to organize all of your facts and information that will support your thesis statement.

Day 16   2 Objectives

*Write your introductory paragraph. Remember to start out with an "attention grabber". See #6 under "HOW TO WRITE A PERSUASIVE ESSAY" for ideas for an attention grabber. *Write your thesis statement as the last sentence in your introductory paragraph.

Day 17   6 Objectives

*Write the body paragraphs of your essay. In these paragraphs, *prove your thesis statement by supporting it with specific *facts*, *details*, *examples*, and *quotes*. *Each paragraph must begin with a topic sentence that *supports* your thesis statement. *Each paragraph must end with a concluding sentence that *summarizes* the paragraph. *Make sure that each body paragraph starts with transition words such as "First", "Next", "Lastly", etc. *If you are *describing* something or someone in your expository essay, make sure that you have included enough *specific* **nouns** and *descriptive* **adjectives**, **verbs**, and **adverbs**.

Day 18   2 Objectives

*Start to write your concluding paragraph by *restating* (in different words) the thesis statement that you wrote in your introductory paragraph.

⇒ Do not start your concluding paragraph by saying, "In conclusion...." or "I will conclude by saying...." Write your sentence without a reference to "conclusion".

⇒ Also, do not introduce any new fact or idea in your conclusion. A conclusion concludes and does not introduce.

*<u>End</u> this concluding paragraph by *leaving* your readers with a fact, quote or example about your topic that will <u>not</u> <u>be</u> <u>easy</u> for them to forget.

Day 19 6 Objectives

*Read your entire essay out loud to someone or have someone read it aloud to you. *Listen for <u>clarity</u> of your *thesis statement* and <u>clarity</u> of *focus*. *Make sure that you have *clearly* <u>proven</u> <u>your</u> <u>point</u>. *Make sure that you have sufficient examples and facts to *thoroughly* <u>explain</u> <u>your</u> <u>topic</u>. If you are describing something, *make sure that you have several *specific* **nouns** and *descriptive* **adjectives**, **verbs**, and **adverbs**. *Proofread your essay using the proofreading checklists on pages 108 and 114.

Day 20 3 Objectives

*Rewrite or type your essay. *Read your finished copy to someone. *Place it in your portfolio.

UNIT 5

WRITING A LITERARY CRITIQUE AND A BOOK REVIEW

Please Note: This unit is four weeks long.

LITERARY CRITIQUES – DAYS 1 through 10

Background: At one point in his career, Edgar Allan Poe was a literary critic. Andrew Lang, Scotland's "Man of Letters", took the position that Mr. Poe's literary abilities and accomplishments were too high for him to have spent his time critiquing literature. (In fact, Lang thought that Mr. Poe was arguably, the greatest poet America had produced – quite a conviction!) Coming from such a literary man as Mr. Lang, this conclusion underscores Mr. Poe's broad and effective abilities regarding literary criticism.

Day 1 4 Objectives (each objective is indicated by an asterisk)

*Read the definition of a literary critique on page 96. *Read this literary critique by Edgar Allan Poe of Nathaniel Hawthorne's *Twice-Told Tales*. *As you read, look up any unfamiliar words in your dictionary such as "titular" and "surfeit" to help you understand Mr. Poe. He wrote in the middle 1800's. *If you are not familiar with Nathaniel Hawthorne and his writings, look him up in an encyclopedia, other book, or on the Internet.

Critique of
Twice-Told Tales

Graham's Magazine April 1842

We have always regarded the *Tale* (using this word in its popular acceptation) as affording the best prose opportunity for display of the highest talent. It has peculiar advantages which the novel does not admit. It is, of course, a far finer field than the essay. It has even points of superiority over the poem. With rare exception--in the case of Mr. Irving's "Tales of a Traveller" and a few other works of a like cast--we have had no American tales of high merit. We have had no skilful compositions--nothing which could bear examination as works of art. Of twattle called tale-writing we have had, perhaps, more than enough. We have had a superabundance of the Rosa-Matilda effusions--gilt-edged paper all rosy colored: a full allowance of cut-and-thrust blue-blazing melodramaticisms; a nauseating surfeit of low miniature copying of low life, much in the manner, and with about half the merit, of the Dutch herrings and decayed cheeses of Van Tuyssel!

Mr. Hawthorne's volumes appear to us misnamed in two respects. In the first place they should not have been called "Twice-Told Tales"--for this is a title which will not bear *repetition*. If in the first collected edition they were twice-told, of course now they are thrice-told.--May we live to hear them told a hundred times! In the second place, these compositions are by no means *all* "Tales". The most of them are essays properly so called. It would have been wise in their author to have modified his title, so as to have had reference to all included. This point could have been easily arranged.

But under whatever titular blunders we receive this book, it is most cordially welcome. We have seen no prose composition by any American which can compare with *some* of these articles in the higher merits, or indeed in the lower; while there is not a single piece which would do dishonor to the best of the British essayists.

"The Rill from the Town Pump" which, through the nature of its title, has attracted more of public notice than any one other of Mr. Hawthorne's compositions, is perhaps, the least meritorious. Among his best, we may briefly mention "The Hollow of the Three Hills", "The Minister's Black Veil", "Wakefield", "Mr. Higginbotham's Catastrophe", "Fancy's Show-Box", "Dr. Heidegger's Experiment", "David Swan", "The Wedding Knell", and "The White Old Maid". It is remarkable that all these, with one exception, are from the first volume.

The style of Mr. Hawthorne is purity itself. His tone is singularly effective--wild, plaintive, thoughtful, and in full accordance with his themes. We have only to object that there is insufficient diversity in these themes themselves, or rather in their character. His originality both of incident and of reflection is very remarkable; and this trait alone would ensure him at least our warmest regard and commendation. We speak here chiefly of the tales; the essays are not so markedly novel. Upon the whole we look upon him as one of the few men of indisputable genius to whom our country has as yet given birth. As such, it will be our delight to do him honor; and lest, in these undigested and cursory remarks, we should appear to do him more honor than is his due, we postpone all farther comment until a more favorable opportunity.

Day 2 3 Objectives

*Read Mr. Poe's critique again. *What does Mr. Poe see as Hawthorne's strengths? Write these down. *What does he list as Hawthorne's weaknesses? List these too.

Day 3 4 Objectives

*Read "HOW TO WRITE A LITERARY CRITIQUE AND A BOOK REVIEW" in the "HOW TO WRITE GUIDE" on pages 96-98. *<u>Make</u> <u>sure</u> that you understand it <u>thoroughly</u>. *What *specific* literary aspect(s) of Hawthorne's does Mr. Poe analyze? (For example: his tone, his style, his themes, etc.) *Write down what he says about these.

Day 4 5 Objectives

*Read Mr. Poe's introductory paragraph again and pay special attention to *how* he writes his introduction. *What "attention grabber" does he use to make his points?

⇒ The thesis statement of a literary critique gives the main point(s) about the important feature(s) under analysis such as theme, imagery, etc.

*What is Mr. Poe's thesis statement? **After** you complete this objective, see the special note on page 119 in the answer key under Day 4. *Choose a literary work that you will do a critique on. <u>Make</u> <u>sure</u> that you choose one that you are <u>very</u> <u>familiar</u> <u>with</u> or that you have <u>strong</u> <u>feelings</u> <u>about</u>.

- Parents and students: I've instructed students to write according to strong feelings that they have because it makes learning to write this genre easier if they have strong feelings about their subject matter.

You can choose a novel, biography or autobiography, short story, essay, poem, play, or article.

Day 5   4 Objectives

*Write down *everything* that you know about the literary work that you chose yesterday – the things that you like and don't like. *Write down the <u>main</u> <u>things</u> that *grab your attention* about this work. Look back over the selection for information if you need to. *Choose a *specific aspect* of the literary work that you would like to critique or analyze such as a character, the plot, theme, setting, style, or imagery. *From this information, come up with your thesis statement. Remember, your thesis statement gives the main point(s) that you are trying to make about the important feature that you are analyzing such as theme, imagery, etc.

Day 6   1 Objective

*Write an outline of everything that you will cover in your critique. Choose either a topical or sentence outline.

Day 7 3 Objectives

*Start your introduction. The first sentence should state the *title*, *author*, and *type* of literary work that you are analyzing. For example: "*The Woodlands* by Robert Smith is a novel about a small town in Texas." *Next, decide on an "attention grabber" such as a quotation or some background information. If you use a quote, comment on its <u>importance</u> *in relation to* your thesis statement. If you use background information, make sure that it is <u>interesting</u> <u>enough</u> to *arrest* your readers.

*Now put your thesis statement from Day 5 at the <u>end</u> of the introductory paragraph.

Day 8 2 Objectives

Today you will write the *body* of your critique. *<u>Make</u> <u>sure</u> that the following elements are found in the body:

- Each body paragraph must support your thesis statement.
- Each paragraph must begin with a topic sentence that supports your thesis statement.
- Your body paragraphs must also contain specific details or quotes <u>from</u> <u>the</u> <u>literary</u> <u>work</u> that you are analyzing in order to prove your points.
- You must not simply state your opinion without giving these specific details or quotes.

*Write your body paragraphs.

Day 9 3 Objectives

Today you will write your *concluding* paragraph. *Begin your conclusion by restating (stating again in different words) your thesis statement that

Diagnostic Prescriptive Services

you wrote in your introductory paragraph. *Make sure that you also include a final unforgettable thought or a "clincher" about the piece that you are critiquing. Once again, this can be a quote, an interesting fact about the work, background information, or an example from the work itself. *End this paragraph with a concluding sentence.

Day 10 5 Objectives

*Read "HOW TO WRITE A LITERARY CRITIQUE AND A BOOK REVIEW" on pages 96-98 again. *<u>Make</u> <u>sure</u> that you have included <u>all</u> of the elements that you need in your critique. *Next, proofread your literary critique using the proofreading checklists on pages 109 and 114. *Write or type your final copy. *Place your final copy in your writing portfolio, with a copy of the literary work that you analyzed, if possible.

BOOK REVIEWS – DAYS 11 through 20

Day 11   2 Objectives

*Read this review by William Dean Howells of Mark Twain's book *The Adventures of Tom Sawyer*.

*As you read, write the definitions of any unfamiliar words.

Book Review of
The Adventures of Tom Sawyer
Atlantic Monthly May 1876

Mr. Clemens has taken the boy of the Southwest for the hero of his new book, and has presented him with a fidelity to circumstance which loses no charm by being realistic in the highest degree, and which gives incomparably the best picture of life in that region as yet known to fiction. The town where Tom Sawyer was born and brought up is some such idle, shabby little Mississippi River town as Mr. Clemens has so well described in his piloting reminiscences, but Tom belongs to the better sort of people in it, and has been bred to fear God and dread the Sunday-school according to the strictest rite of the faiths that have characterized all the respectability of the West. His subjection in these respects does not so deeply affect his inherent tendencies but that he makes himself a beloved burden to the poor tender-hearted old aunt who brings him up with his orphan brother and sister, and struggles vainly with his manifold sins, actual and imaginary. The limitations of his transgressions are nicely and artistically traced. He is mischievous, but not vicious; he is ready for almost any depredation that involves the danger and honor of adventure, but profanity he knows may provoke a thunderbolt upon the heart of the blasphemer and he almost never swears; he resorts to any stratagem to keep out of school, but he is not a downright liar, except upon terms of shame and remorse, and these make his falsehood bitter to him. He is cruel, as all children are, but chiefly because he is ignorant; he is not mean, but there are very definite bounds to his generosity; and his courage is the Indian sort, full of prudence and mindful of retreat as one of the conditions of prolonged hostilities. In a word, he is a boy, and merely and exactly an ordinary boy on the moral side. What makes him delightful to the reader is that on the imaginative side he is very much more, and though every boy has wild and fantastic dreams, this boy cannot rest till he has somehow realized them. Till he has actually run off with two other boys in the character of buccaneer, and lived for a week on an island in the Mississippi, he has lived in vain; and this passage is but the prelude to more thrilling adventures, in which he finds hidden treasures, traces the bandits to their cave, and is himself lost in its recesses. The local material and the incidents with which his career is worked up are excellent, and throughout there is scrupulous regard for the boy's point of view in reference to his surroundings and himself, which shows how rapidly Mr. Clemens has grown as an artist. We do not remember anything in which this propriety is violated, and its preservation adds immensely to the grownup reader's satisfaction in the amusing and exciting story. There is a boy's love-affair, but it is never treated otherwise than as a boy's love-affair. When the half-breed has murdered the young doctor, Tom and his friend, Huckleberry Finn, are really, in their boyish terror and superstition, going to let the poor old town-drunkard be hanged for the crime till the terror of that becomes unendurable. The story is a wonderful study of the boy-mind, which inhabits a world quite distinct from that in which he is bodily present with his elders, and in this lies its great charm and its universality, for boy nature, however human nature varies, is the same everywhere.

The tale is very dramatically wrought, and the subordinate characters are treated with the same graphic force that sets Tom alive before us. The worthless vagabond, Huck Finn, is entirely delightful throughout, and in his promised reform his identity is respected: he will lead a decent life in order that he may one day be thought worthy to become a member of that gang of robbers which Tom is to organize. Tom's aunt is excellent, with her kind heart's sorrow and secret pride in Tom; and so is his sister Mary, one of those good girls who are born to usefulness and charity and forbearance and unvarying rectitude. Many village people and local notables are introduced in well-conceived character; the whole little town lives in the reader's sense, with its religiousness, its lawlessness, its droll social distinctions, its civilization qualified by its slaveholding, and its traditions of the wilder West which has passed away. The picture will be instructive to those who have fancied the whole Southwest a sort of vast Pike County, and have not conceived of a sober and serious and orderly contrast to the sort of life that has come to represent the Southwest in literature. Mr. Clemens has again enforced the fact here in a book full of entertaining character and of the greatest artistic sincerity.

Day 12 4 Objectives

*Carefully read "HOW TO WRITE A LITERARY CRITIQUE AND A BOOK REVIEW" on pages 96-98 again, paying special attention to #'s 4, 5, 6, and 8. *According to Mr. Howells' first sentence, what *specific aspects* of the book *The Adventures of Tom Sawyer* does he focus on when writing his review? *Does Mr. Howells cover these aspects *thoroughly*? *Write some specific examples of the way that he thoroughly covers these elements of the book. For example, what does he say about Tom's character and the setting? How does Mr. Howells talk about his characters and the setting?

Day 13 6 Objectives

*Looking at Mr. Howells' review again, underline his "attention grabber". *Rewrite Mr. Howells' attention grabber in your own words. *Does he *adequately* summarize the book by giving *details* about the plot? *Does he give the readers his opinion of the book? (Keep in mind, that Mr. Howells did not follow our modern rules or guidelines as to where or how to summarize the plot or give his opinion of the book.) *What is Mr. Howells' opinion of *The Adventures of Tom Sawyer?* *Write this in your own words.

Day 14   7 Objectives

*Choose a book that you really like, are very familiar with and preferably, have recently read.
> Note: Make sure that you ask your teacher because she may have a book in mind that she wants you to review. This is a good time to combine subjects and perhaps review a biography or historical fiction book that you have read or are reading.

*Write down *all* of your thoughts about this book. *List the main parts or features of the book that impressed you such as *descriptive* language, *realistic* characters, action, etc. Read over the book again if you need to. *List *all* of the things that you like and do not like about the book. *Read your entries from objectives 2 through 4 above and *circle* the points that you will include in your book review. *Compare your lists for similarities (points of comparison) to Mr. Howells' details as covered under days 12 and 13 above. Are your lists adequate? *If not, redo them until they are as detailed as his are.

Day 15   5 Objectives

*Arrive at your thesis statement. *Write this down.
⇒ This sentence must tell about the main part of the book that made an impression on you either in a positive or negative way.

This can be something that you learned from the book or something that you think others could learn from it. For example, if you were impressed with the theme of Nathaniel Hawthorne's *The Scarlet Letter,* you could write, "Through Hester Pryne's ordeal in Puritan New England, one can learn what hypocrisy truly is and how very important honesty and forgiveness are." *Start writing your introductory paragraph. Your first sentence must *state the title, author, and theme or subject of the book that you are reviewing. Also, *state the type of book that you are reviewing such as a novel, historical novel, biography, autobiography, nonfiction, etc. in the first sentence.

Day 16 2 Objectives

*Decide on an "attention grabber" to gain the attention of your readers. You can use some background information about the book, the author, or time period of the setting of the book or a quotation from the book itself. You can also ask the readers a question to gain attention.
Work carefully on this because of its particular importance.
⇒ Remember that an attention grabber is any relevant device used to *arrest* the interest of the reader.
*Conclude your introductory paragraph, and use your thesis statement arrived at yesterday as its last sentence.

Day 17 2 Objectives

Over the next two days you will write the *body* paragraphs of your book review. The body should be two or more paragraphs long. The first paragraph must be a summary of the main points of the book. *Read entry #6 under "HOW TO WRITE A LITERARY CRITIQUE AND A BOOK REVIEW" on page 97 again. *Write your summary paragraph – the first body paragraph.

Day 18   2 Objectives

*Write your other body paragraph or paragraphs. This paragraph or these paragraphs must support your thesis statement made in your introductory paragraph. For example, if you are writing about the theme in *The Scarlet Letter* (as seen on Day 15), you must give *specific examples* of Hester's "ordeal" to show how readers can learn about hypocrisy, honesty, and forgiveness. *Make sure to use *details*, *examples*, and/or *quotations* to support your opinion.

Day 19   3 Objectives

Today you will write the concluding paragraph of your book review. *Begin by writing the *topic sentence* of this paragraph. It will state your *opinion* about the book – whether you liked it or disliked it and whether you would recommend it to someone else for reading. *Continue this paragraph by giving *specific details* about why you liked or disliked the book. These details can include facts about the characters, action, setting, dialogue or descriptive language used by the author. *End your paragraph with a concluding sentence that restates your topic sentence *in different words*.

Day 20   2 Objectives

*Proofread your book review using the proofreading checklists on pages 110 and 114. *Rewrite or type your final copy, and place it in your portfolio.

www.edudps.com

UNIT 6

WRITING A NEWSPAPER ARTICLE

Background: In his early writing career, Ernest Hemingway was a reporter for the *Kansas City Star.* He viewed this experience as highly beneficial to his later writing career.

Day 1   2 Objectives (each objective is indicated by an asterisk)

*Read this newspaper article by Mr. Hemingway.

WOULD 'TREAT 'EM ROUGH'

Kansas City Star

April 18, 1918

Four men stood outside the army recruiting office at Twelfth Street and Grand Avenue at 7:45 o'clock this morning when the sergeant opened up. A stout, red faced man wearing a khaki shirt was the first up the stairs.

"I'm the treat 'em rough man," he bawled. "That cat in the poster has nothing on me. Where do you join the tankers?"

"Have to wait for Lieutenant Cooter," said the sergeant. "He decides whether you'll treat 'em rough or not."

The fat man waited outside the door. By 9 o'clock thirty men crowded the third floor hallway. The stout man was nearest the door. Just behind him was a gray haired man wearing a derby, a well cut gray suit, a purple tie, socks to match and a silk handkerchief with a light purple border peeping from his vest pocket.

"I'm over draft age and it doesn't matter what my profession is," he said. "I never really wanted to get into this war before, but the tanks are different. I guess I can treat 'em rough."

The crowd grew steadily. By 10 o'clock there were forty applicants. Some of the men were humming, others talking among themselves. The stout man, perspiration pouring down his face, held his place next to the door. He tried to whistle, but his lips wouldn't pucker. He stood on one foot, then the other. He mopped his face with a handkerchief, and finally bolted out through the crowd.

"He looked pretty hot, but he got cold feet," a mechanic in overalls commented.

After the fat man left there was a slight exodus. A high school boy with a geometry book decided in favor of school.

Two flashily dressed youths said, "Aw, let's get a beer." One man, saying nothing, slipped away.

"Can't stand the gaff," said the mechanic.

But most of the applicants stayed.

A youth wearing an army shirt explained: "It's my girl. I belonged to the home guards and she kind of kidded me. Nobody's going to kid a tanker, I guess."

The opinion of most of the men was voiced by a clerk. "I don't know anything about tractors or machinery, but I can learn to work a machine gun, and I want to get across. Gee, I hope I get in."

A little man with double lens glasses said: "I don't suppose they'll take me. Guess I'm pretty useless. But I want to try. It's about my last chance. They all throw me down."

When Lieut. Frank E. Cooter, special tank recruiting officer, appeared, the crowd formed a line outside the door. The men were admitted one at a time. Moistening their lips, they entered the little room and stated their qualifications. John R. Ecklund, 27 years old, was one of the first admitted.

"What mechanical experience have you had?" he was asked.

"None. I'm an attorney for the Kansas City Street Railways Company," he replied.

"Why do you want to join?"

"I want to see action and get over in a hurry."

Lieutenant Cooter accepted him.

"That is the type of all of them," the lieutenant said. "That is what brings men here. Not promises of high pay or easy service, but telling the truth about quick action and danger. 'To know and yet to dare,' would be a good slogan. Quick service, quick promotion and action, action, is what brings them. They are the finest type of men for soldiers."

Besides Ecklund, six other men were accepted for service up to noon.

*Circle all *specific* **nouns**, and underline all *descriptive* **verbs** in green, all *descriptive* **adjectives** in red, and all *descriptive* **adverbs** in blue.

Day 2   4 Objectives

*Read Mr. Hemingway's newspaper article again.

*What event is the author describing? Write down the answer. *With a red or other colored fine point marker, go through the article and underline the sentences that answer these questions about the event that Mr. Hemingway describes:

   Who?

   What?

   When?

   Where?

   Why?

   How?

I call these questions the six pithy NA (newspaper article) questions.

*Write the six word questions next to the sentences to which they apply.

Day 3   6 Objectives

*Read "HOW TO WRITE A NEWSPAPER ARTICLE" on page 99.
*Looking back at Mr. Hemingway's article, what is the *main idea* or *focus* of his article? In other words, under(what) is he trying to say to his readers? **How* does Mr. Hemingway get his main focus or idea across? *Underline Mr. Hemingway's "attention grabber". *Is his attention grabber properly placed in his article? *Is his title focused, brief, and eye-catching?

Day 4   5 Objectives

*Come up with an event that you will write a newspaper article about. (Your teacher may suggest that you pick an important event in history or science that you are studying presently or have studied before.) *Write down everything that you know about this event. If it is an event where you were actually present, write down the *sights*, *sounds*, and *smells* that you remember. Remember the techniques that you learned in Volume 1 and describe your sights, sounds, and smells as though you were having to describe these things to someone who couldn't see, hear, and smell. *Make it your purpose* to use <u>vivid</u> descriptions while *avoiding* generic descriptions. If you weren't present, use your imagination and think about the sights, sounds, and smells that may have been present at such an event. Write these down. *Arrive at one main idea or feeling that you want to *focus* on in your article. *What is it* that you want to say to your readers about this event? Be <u>very</u> <u>clear</u> about this. *Write down this main idea or focus.

Day 5   2 Objectives

*Referring back to the sights, sounds, and smells that you wrote down yesterday, use your thesaurus and add or substitute some *specific* **nouns** and *descriptive* **verbs**, **adjectives**, and **adverbs** that will <u>help give support</u> to the description of your event. *Use some conversation between or among people who were involved in the event. (See *WRITE WITH THE BEST Vol. 1* - "HOW TO WRITE A DIALOGUE" for rules on how to write conversation.)

Day 6   2 Objectives

*Thinking about the event that you will describe, answer the six pithy NA questions <u>using</u> *specific* **nouns** and *descriptive* **adjectives**, **verbs**, and **adverbs**. (Remember, <u>avoid</u> using generic and uninteresting parts of speech. Use your thesaurus.) Again, they are:

    Who?

    What?

When?

Where?

Why?

How?

*Write down the answers to these six questions.

Day 7   4 Objectives

Today you will start writing your article.

Start writing your article, and *quickly use an "attention grabber". Like Mr. Hemingway, you may want to use a few sentences first that utilize full description, and then use dialogue as your attention grabber. Mr. Hemingway makes sure that he gives us visual word pictures at the start of his article to help us see the event that he is describing. He fully describes his first candidate and puts his attention grabber in his mouth. By doing so, he grabs his readers *right from the start.* *Continue by writing the body of your article, making certain that your *main idea* is clearly communicated throughout. *Be sure to incorporate the answers to the six questions of yesterday. *Include interesting dialogue if you are able to.

Day 8   3 Objectives

*Conclude your newspaper article today by *summing up* the main points about the event that you are describing. *Also, make sure that your main idea or focus is *clearly* restated in your summary. Restate your main idea or focus using *different words* than you used in the body of your article. Consider following Mr. Hemingway by using a conversation to sum up the event. Note that in an effective way, he summarized his article with conversation. *Come up with a good title for your article. **Note:** Your title should state the main idea or focus of your article, should be concise, and should be "catchy", meaning that it should catch or grab the reader's attention when he reads it.

Day 9 2 Objectives

*Proofread your entire article today using the proofreading checklists on pages 111 and 114. *<u>Make</u> <u>sure</u> that while your article is *concise* and *to the point*, it <u>thoroughly</u> answers the six pithy NA questions.

Day 10 2 Objectives

*Rewrite or type your final article. *Place this in your portfolio.
Note: If your local homeschool or school group has a newsletter, consider putting your newspaper article in the newsletter. You could also make your own "Family Newsletter". Many homeschool families like to send family newsletters out at Christmas time.

UNIT 7

WRITING A SPEECH

Background: I need to supply some historical information about this speech to enable you to understand it.

In the latter years of the Roman republic, the senate formulated a decree called the *senatus consultum ultimum.* This "ultimate decree of the senate" was designed as an emergency measure that enabled rulers to quickly take whatever action was deemed necessary for the defense of Rome against her enemies, both real and supposed. Any action, including the death penalty, could be taken without strictly holding to legal procedure. While this decree had the positive effect of immediately terminating harm to the state, it also lent itself to great abuse. In 100 BC, a man named L. Appuleius Saturninus was arrested under the decree. While he was being held as a prisoner in the senate-house, a mob attacked and killed him. A prominent figure among the mob was Gaius Rabirius. Some time later – about forty years later – Julius Caesar determined to impugn the senatorial decree. He decided to hold up the abuses of the decree as a method of attacking and undermining its legality. Gaius Rabirius, who was then an aged, backseat senator, was ready at hand. In order to reveal what a bad decree could do in the hands of would-be decent men, Caesar dusted off an old law and had Rabirius prosecuted for the murder of Saturninus. Cicero, who was for the decree, notwithstanding its potential abuses, was Rabirius' defender. That was not the only time that Cicero went head-to-head with Caesar regarding the enforcement of the emergency decree. Although the decree isn't specifically named in Cicero's speech, it is referred to as "that great aid". I have, accordingly, italicized the phrase in the text. Lastly, the speeches of the ancient orators were very long. I have, therefore, condensed this speech of Cicero's. Marcus Tullius Cicero is considered by many to be the greatest orator of ancient Rome.

Day 1 3 Objectives (each objective is indicated by an asterisk)

*Read the following excerpt from "In Defense of Rabirius – Before the Senate" by Marcus Tullius Cicero. *Underline any unfamiliar words while reading. *Look up these words, and write down their definitions.

IN DEFENSE OF RABIRIUS – BEFORE THE SENATE

Although, O Romans, it is not my custom at the beginning of a speech to give any reason why I am defending each particular defendant, because I have always considered that the mere fact of the danger of any citizen was quite sufficient reason for my considering myself connected with him, still, in this instance, when I come forward to defend the life, and character, and all the fortunes of Gaius Rabirius, I think I ought to give reasons for my undertaking this duty; because the very same reasons which have appeared to me as most adequate to prompt me to undertake his defense, ought also to appear to you sufficient to induce you to acquit him. For the ancientness of my friendship with him, and the dignity of the man, and a regard for humanity, and the uninterrupted practice of my life, have instigated me to defend Gaius Rabirius; and also my duty as consul, the safety of the republic, and also that of each individual citizen in it as entrusted to me, compel me to do so with the greatest zeal. For it is not the actual offence, nor any desire to deprive Gaius Rabirius in particular of life, nor is it any old, well grounded, serious enmity on the part of any citizen, which has brought him into this peril of his life. But the true design of this prosecution is, that *that great aid* which the majesty of the state and our dominion enjoys, and which has been handed down to us from our ancestors, may be banished from the republic; that the authority of the senate, and the absolute power of the consul, and the unanimity of all good men, may henceforth be of no avail against any mischief or ruin designed to the state; and therefore, as a handle for the destruction of all these weighty obstacles, the old age, and infirmity, and solitary condition of one man is attacked.

Wherefore, if it is the part of a virtuous consul when he sees all the bulwarks of the republic undermined and weakened, to come to the assistance of his country; to bring succour to the safety and fortunes of all men; to implore the good faith of the citizens; to think his own safety of secondary consideration when put in competition with the common safety of all; it is the part also of virtuous and fearless citizens, such as you have shown yourselves to be in all the emergencies of the republic, to block up all the avenues of sedition, to fortify the bulwarks of the state, to think that the supreme power is vested in the consuls, the supreme wisdom in the senate; and to judge the man who acts in obedience to them, worthy of praise and honour, rather than of condemnation and punishment. Wherefore the labour in defending this man falls principally to my share; but the zeal for his preservation ought to be equally felt by me and by you. For you ought to think, O Romans, that, in the memory of man, no affair more important, more full of peril to you, more necessary to be carefully watched by you, has ever been undertaken by a tribune of the people, nor opposed by a consul, nor brought before the Roman people. For there is nothing less at stake, O Romans, in this than there is in any other like object, than the preventing of any public council from being active for the future in the republic, any union from being formed of good men against the frenzy and insanity of wicked citizens; any refuge, any protection, any safety from existing at the most critical extremity of the republic.

And, as this is the case, in the first place, as is most necessary to be done, in such a contest for a man's life and reputation, and all his fortunes, I entreat pardon and indulgence. I pray that this day may have dawned for the salvation of this man, and for the welfare of the republic. And, in the second place, I beg and entreat you, O Romans,--you whose power comes nearest to the divine authority of the immortal gods,--that since at one and the same time the life of Gaius Rabirius, a most unhappy and most innocent man, and the safety of the republic is entrusted to your hands and to your votes, you will display that mercy, as far as regards the fortunes of the individual, and that wisdom in what concerns the safety of the republic, which you are accustomed to exercise.

Day 2 4 Objectives

*Read "HOW TO WRITE A SPEECH" on pages 100-101. *Read Cicero's "In Defense of Rabirius – Before the Senate" again. *Write down in *your own words* what Cicero is saying.

Day 3 4 Objectives

*Answer this question – Has Cicero written his speech to inform, persuade, or show someone how to do something? *<u>Underline</u> in red the sentence or sentences that show Cicero's purpose for his speech (his thesis statement). *<u>Underline</u> Cicero's "attention grabber" in blue. *Rewrite his attention grabber using your own words.

Day 4 4 Objectives

*Referring to Cicero's speech again, list 7 ways that he persuades his audience. Has Cicero persuaded <u>you</u>? *If not, write down other ways or points of persuasion that you would have used in this situation. *<u>Underline</u> Cicero's "attention grabber" in his conclusion. *Does Cicero's conclusion restate his most important points, explain the importance of these points, and call his audience to action?

Day 5 4 Objectives

Choose a topic that you will write a speech on or ask your teacher for a topic. *Choose a topic that you are really interested in or are very familiar with. *Decide whether you will persuade, inform, explain, or demonstrate something to your audience. *Collect and list <u>all</u> of the information that you will need to write your speech. Remember that you will need <u>sufficient</u> facts and details to support the kind of speech that you have chosen. *After collecting all of your information, write your thesis statement. Remember, your *thesis statement* must tell what your whole speech will be about and the purpose of your speech. **Note:** Unlike an essay or literary critique, a thesis statement for a speech will start by saying, "My purpose is to persuade, explain, etc." Start this thesis statement by saying, "The purpose of my speech is to persuade you to" or "The purpose of my speech is to explain to you how to", etc.

Day 6 2 Objectives

*Take all of the information that you have gathered so far and arrange it into a sentence outline. (See "HOW TO WRITE AN OUTLINE" on pages 87-90. for help.) *Work on your outline until you have included all of the important points that you will make in your speech.

Day 7 4 Objectives

*Write the introduction to your speech. The introduction is particularly important. *Start it with an "attention grabber". (See #6 on page 93 for ideas for attention grabbers.) *After you write the attention grabber, introduce your topic by giving a few details about it, and then *end the introduction with your thesis statement. **Note:** In speeches, attention grabbers generally come before the topic is introduced.

Day 8 10 Objectives

*Write the body paragraphs of your speech. *You must have *one* paragraph for *each* main point that you are making. *Your *points* must relate to your *thesis statement*. Refer to your sentence outline for help with the body paragraphs. Each paragraph must *start with a *topic sentence* and *end with a *concluding sentence*. *Use transition words at the beginnings of separate paragraphs so that they flow together. *Write the conclusion for your speech. *Start your conclusion with another "attention grabber" such as a short story or interesting fact. *Sum up the *main points* of your speech in your conclusion. *End your conclusion by telling your audience again why the topic that you have chosen is significant and whether you or they should and/or will take any action concerning what you have related to them.

Day 9   4 Objectives

*Read your speech out loud, preferably to someone else. *Make sure that you have related your topic *efficiently* and have stuck to your subject and thesis statement. *Make sure that the purpose of your speech is *clear* and that you have *fulfilled that purpose* by providing the required supporting facts. For example, if you have written a speech to persuade your audience about an opinion, have you given enough information to persuade them? If you have written a speech to inform your audience of something, does your speech have sufficient details? *Proofread your speech using the proofreading checklists on pages 112 and 114.

Day 10   3 Objectives

*Rewrite or type the final draft of your speech, and *place it in your portfolio. *Practice giving this speech out loud in front of your family or a group of friends.

Note: Homeschoolers are not often given a lot of opportunities to give speeches or speak in front of an audience, and these are skills that can be very beneficial. You may choose to use your written speech or your outline in giving your speech. Make sure that you practice it sufficiently before standing before your audience so that you don't have to look down at your paper too much.

UNIT 8

WRITING A DRAMATIC MONOLOGUE

Concerning Dramatic Monologues: There is presently notable discussion about dramatic monologues among writers and analysts regarding the "invention", definition, and interpretation of the genre. Some of these contend that dramatic monologues were invented and developed by certain Victorian Age poets and require specific features, some actually being aspects of soliloquy, to qualify them as dramatic monologues. In fact, the definition of the genre is broader than that adhered to by this group. Likewise, its origin is considerably before the nineteenth century. It is interesting – and telling – to see the genre defined differently among various sources and even to witness change of definition within like sources from time to time. This, in itself, attests to the differences of opinion that are currently held by these writers and literary analysts. I subscribe to the earlier, larger, and basic definition of dramatic monologue for the purposes of writing and this curriculum.

⇒ **Dramatic monologue:** an uninterrupted talk of relative length made by a character in a dramatic situation and in the presence of an audience, real or imaginary, about himself, the situation itself and/or other characters involved in it. In this talk, characteristics, motives, emotions, events, and/or facts are revealed.

Day 1   5 Objectives (each objective is indicated by an asterisk)

*To better understand the background and purpose of Shakespeare's dramatic monologue, discover who Julius Caesar, Mark Antony, and Brutus were. *Read the dramatic monologue given by the character Mark Antony in William Shakespeare's play *Julius Caesar*. *Write down the definitions of any unfamiliar words.

JULIUS CAESAR

ANTONY:

Friends, Romans, countrymen, lend me your ears;

I come to bury Caesar, not to praise him.

The evil that men do lives after them;

The good is oft interred with their bones:

So let it be with Caesar. The noble Brutus

Hath told you Caesar was ambitious:

If it were so, it was a grievous fault;

And grievously hath Caesar answer'd it.

Here, under leave of Brutus and the rest,--

For Brutus is an honourable man;

So are they all, all honorable men,--

Come I to speak in Caesar's funeral.

He was my friend, faithful and just to me:

But Brutus says he was ambitious;

And Brutus is an honourable man.

He hath brought many captives home to Rome,

Whose ransoms did the general coffers fill:

Did this in Caesar seem ambitious?

When that the poor have cried, Caesar hath wept:

Ambition should be made of sterner stuff:

Yet Brutus says he was ambitious;

And Brutus is an honourable man.

You all did see that on the Lupercal

I thrice presented him a kingly crown,

Which he did thrice refuse: was this ambition?

Yet Brutus says he was ambitious;

And, sure, he is an honourable man.

I speak not to disprove what Brutus spoke,

But here I am to speak what I do know.

You all did love him once,--not without cause:

What cause withholds you, then, to mourn for him?--

O judgment, thou art fled to brutish beasts,

And men have lost their reason!--Bear with me;

My heart is in the coffin there with Caesar,

And I must pause till it come back to me.

What do you think that Mr. Shakespeare is saying to his readers through this dramatic monologue? *Write down his main focus or theme. (See *WRITE WITH THE BEST Vol. 1* page 37 for the explanation of theme.) *Write down the occasion of this monologue.

Day 2 6 Objectives

*Why do you think that playwrights include dramatic monologues in plays? *After you answer this question, see page 123, Day 2 – first bullet item only. *Read the monologue by Mr. Shakespeare again. *What is Shakespeare saying about Mark Antony through his monologue? *What does he want his audience to know about Brutus and Julius Caesar? *Underline two examples of personification in the last four lines. (See Unit 1, page 17, for the definition of personification.)

Day 3 3 Objectives

*Circle all *specific* **nouns**, and underline *descriptive* **adjectives** in red and **verbs** in green in Shakespeare's dramatic monologue. *Write down the answers to the following questions: (1) *Why* does Mark Antony repeat "honourable" so often? (2) *What* is Shakespeare trying to say to the audience by doing this? (3) *How* does he gain the attention of his readers in the opening of the monologue? (4) *What* is the conflict or problem that the monologue is built around? (5) *How* does Shakespeare end the dramatic monologue in a way that the audience will not forget? *Read "HOW TO WRITE A DRAMATIC MONOLOGUE" on page 102.

Day 4 4 Objectives

*Review the questions and answers from yesterday, as these are effective techniques used by William Shakespeare in a dramatic monologue. *Read #'s 2 and 4 on page 102 again. *Choose a character from a book or story that you have just read or a person you are studying in history. Make sure that he or she was involved in a significant, dramatic event or situation. (A dramatic monologue is sometimes a good alternative for a written book report. You can demonstrate your knowledge and understanding of characters from a book by writing a dramatic monologue for one of the characters.) *Write down *everything* that you can think of about this character or person – his or her personality, actions, etc.

Day 5 7 Objectives

*Decide on the *conflict* that your monologue will be based upon. If your monologue will be by a character in a book that you have read, use a conflict that the character was involved in within the book. If you choose someone from history, use an actual conflict that the person was involved in. *Decide on the facts and details of the dramatic situation that you will bring out in your character's talk. Will they be character traits, emotions, hidden motives or intrigues, etc.? *Write these down. *Decide on the parts of the character's personality from yesterday that you want to express in your <u>dramatic</u> <u>monologue</u>. (For example, his or her bravery, selfishness, egotism, arrogance, loyalty, etc.) *Write these down. *Think about how you will *portray* <u>these</u> <u>parts</u> of your character's personality in a *vivid* way. *Write down some ideas.

Day 6 2 Objectives

*Come up with and write down some *specific* **nouns** and *vivid* **adjectives**, **verbs**, and **adverbs** that you can use to <u>make</u> your <u>monologue</u> "come alive" for your readers. Remember, your aim is to avoid dullness while you supply vivid description to your monologue. Use a dictionary and a thesaurus if you need to. (For extra help with descriptive writing, see *WRITE WITH THE BEST Vol. 1,* Unit 1.) Use some figures of speech like Shakespeare did in your monologue. Think of an example of personification or imagery that you can use. *Write this down.

Day 7 3 Objectives

*Write the beginning or opening of your monologue. *<u>Make</u> <u>sure</u> that you start with something that will grab the attention of your audience. Like Shakespeare, comment about life or death or an *aspect* of life *that relates* to your character <u>and</u> the conflict in which he is involved. Do this in such a way that it will *arrest* your audience. *<u>Make</u> <u>sure</u> that your *theme* is <u>clear</u>.

Day 8 6 Objectives

*Write the main part of your monologue by *revealing* the conflict of your character. *Make sure that you include all of the descriptive and figurative language that you came up with on days 5 and 6. *Make sure that you develop and reveal the details and facts that you wrote down on Day 5. *Make sure that your dramatic monologue is relatively lengthy and that no other character interrupts your main character. One intention of a dramatic monologue is to impact the listeners without interruption. *Write your conclusion. Like Shakespeare, you must end your monologue with a statement that will *remain* in the minds of your readers. *Compare your ending to Shakespeare's. Does your monologue end with a single thought or does it contain a double thought like his does? If you are not satisfied with your ending, use a double thought for a lasting effect.

Day 9 3 Objectives

*Read your finished dramatic monologue out loud to yourself or to someone else. *Verify that your *theme* is clear and that your *audience* clearly understands your character and the dramatic situation after hearing the monologue. *Using the proofreading checklist for a dramatic monologue on page 113, check your monologue for all the necessary components. Use the proofreading checklist on page 114 to check capitalization, punctuation, spelling, and usage.

Day 10 3 Objectives

*Rewrite or type your dramatic monologue. * Read your finished monologue to an audience – the normal setting of a dramatic monologue. This can give you good practice with oratory and dramatic skills. *Place your monologue in your portfolio.

§
LEARNING STYLES SUGGESTIONS
AND OTHER WAYS TO AUGMENT THIS CURRICULUM

Note: When possible, use all the suggestions regarding all learners because this has been proven to help insure retention of the material.

Tactile/Kinesthetic Learners

1. Purchase a large dry-erase board with large red markers for students to use to write their assignments on or to complete other exercises on, such as dictation.
2. To help students understand the literary passages, have them act out the action scenes so that the story comes alive. They may also enjoy and benefit from acting out their own stories.
3. Tactile learners will enjoy drawing pictures to illustrate their writings.
4. Allow these students to type their assignments, if they are able.
5. These learners sometimes have problems with handwriting or putting thoughts on paper, so you may need to do their writing for them as they dictate to you.

Visual Learners

1. Use highlighters and various colors of ink to mark important information in the assignments.
2. These learners will also benefit from proofreading their papers with different colors of ink for different mistakes.

Auditory Learners

1. Auditory learners will enjoy and benefit from narrating (telling the story in their own words) the literary passages back to their teachers.
2. Often it is helpful for these students to first dictate their responses into a tape recorder and then write their assignments from the recording.

General Suggestions

1. Each student should keep a writing portfolio of their final writings with any artistic illustrations they have made to accompany them. Hard-back notebooks (binders) are best for this, but any kind of notebook can be used. This is helpful for students to see the accomplishments and improvements they have made over the school year in their writings.

2. To encourage your students about their writing, I highly recommend that you put on an "Author's Tea" twice a year (around Christmas and in May or June). You can keep this very simple by inviting a few friends and family members and serving simple tea or punch and cookies. Guests are to view all of the "author's" writings and make encouraging comments on comment sheets for the students to keep in their writing portfolios. Students can also read some of their writings out loud to their guests. This is an excellent way to encourage students to write more.

www.edudps.com

ADDITIONAL LITERARY PASSAGES
FOR MODELING WRITING

Teachers please note:

The examples listed below are primarily for the teachers to use as they go through the curriculum <u>again</u> with their students in order to continue to reinforce good writing skills. To use these additional passages, simply substitute them for the original passages included at the beginning of each unit, and <u>use the same daily objectives as guidelines</u>.

Furthermore, I have included some actual literary passages on pages 125-138 because examples of some of the genres taught in this volume are difficult to find. For the additional literary passages listed below, see your public library or bookseller.

Free Verse

- "Chicago" and "Fog" by Carl Sandburg
- "The Negro Speaks of Rivers" by Langston Hughes
- "I, Too" by Langston Hughes
- "All the World's a Stage" from Shakespeare's play *As You Like It*
- "When I Heard the Learn'd Astronomer" and "I Hear America Singing" by Walt Whitman
- "Birches" and "The Pasture" by Robert Frost
- "Paradise Lost" by John Milton
- Poetry of e. e. cummings

Business Letters

- *The Hobbit,* chapter 2, by J. R. R. Tolkien
- "A Petition to Her Majesty, The Queen" by Mark Twain
- See page 125

Essays

- All essays of Francis Bacon

The essays of Ralph Waldo Emerson listed below are mainly for older students because of their difficulty.

- "Nature"
- "Friendship"
- "Compensation"
- "The Morals of Chess" by Benjamin Franklin
- "Of Repentance" by Michel de Montaigne (the beginning of it)

Literary Critiques and Book Reviews

See pages 126-135

Newspaper Articles

See pages 135-138

Speeches

- Speeches of Cicero
- Speeches of Demosthenes
- "The Gettysburg Address" by Abraham Lincoln
- "The Character of Washington" by Daniel Webster
- "A Resolution To Put Virginia Into a State of Defense" by Patrick Henry
- "On Conciliation with the Colonies" by Edmund Burke
- Resignation Speech of George Washington

Dramatic Monologues

- Hamlet's famous monologue in *Hamlet* by Shakespeare (Act III, Scene 1)

- Monologue of Romeo in *Romeo and Juliet* by Shakespeare (Act II, Scene 2 – first monologue)
- Monologue of Macbeth in *Macbeth* by Shakespeare (Act V, Scene 5 – 3rd speech of Macbeth)
- Monologue of Agamemnon in *Agamemnon* by Aeschylus (First lines are: "First to Argos and the country's gods…")
- Monologue of Dawn, wife of King Priam in "The Aeneid" by Virgil (Book IV)

HOW TO WRITE GUIDE

⇒ Read Special Note #1 on page 13 again. It is <u>very</u> <u>important</u> to keep Special Note #1 in mind when using this "HOW TO WRITE GUIDE".

⇒ After completing the curriculum, continue to refer to the "HOW TO WRITE GUIDE" for refreshers and instructions concerning all of your writing needs regarding these genres.

⇒ Also, refer to the "HOW TO WRITE GUIDE" of Vol. 1 for refreshers and needs concerning its genres.

Use your thesaurus to enrich your vocabulary of descriptive and specific language for all of the following genres.

HOW TO WRITE A POEM IN FREE VERSE

1. Think about an idea, opinion, belief, or feeling that you would like to <u>express</u> through a poem, or choose an object, experience, person, place, or memory that you would like to <u>describe</u>. Decide on your theme or message that you will communicate through your poem.

2. Choose the tone of your poem. (See Unit 1 for the definition of tone.)

3. Write down words or phrases that come to mind as you think about the topic that you have chosen. Write as many as you can because this will help you fashion your poem. You need words that will help set the tone of your poem. You should have <u>several</u> vivid or descriptive verbs and adjectives. Adverbs can also be included.

4. Next, write down some figures of speech to use in your poem such as personification or similes. Also use alliteration to add to the sound of your poem.

5. After writing down all of your initial ideas on paper, keep writing and rewriting until every word and line says exactly what you want it to

say. Make sure that you are creating images or pictures in the minds of your readers by using specific, vivid, and descriptive words and phrases.

6. End your poem with an exciting event or an interesting detail.
7. Read your poem out loud or have someone read it to you, and make sure that you can virtually sense the images or pictures that your poem creates.
8. Make sure that the theme or idea that you are trying to get across is clear and developed throughout the poem.
9. Make sure that in the reading of your poem, you hear some kind of rhythm or beat <u>without</u> <u>rhyme</u>.
10. Proofread your poem.

www.edudps.com

HOW TO WRITE A BUSINESS LETTER

1. Determine the purpose or purposes for writing your letter. Do you have a complaint or a request? Do you want to ask someone to do something or inform them of something? Are you applying for something such as a job or scholarship, or are you thanking someone for something in an official manner? Jot down the answers to these questions. This helps focus your intentions.

2. In the beginning paragraph of your letter, *introduce yourself,* and <u>clearly</u> tell the *purpose* of your letter.

3. In the middle or body paragraph, <u>present your information</u> or thoroughly explain your purpose for writing – for example, a thank you if that is your purpose or a request for material, etc., if that is your purpose. *Be specific.* Endeavor to provide interesting details.

4. In the concluding paragraph, your *first sentence* should <u>express</u> your <u>thanks</u> for the consideration of your request, complaint, etc. Next, *state what you expect* the reader to do, if anything, and any time limits, constraints, or other expectations that you may have. For example, if you are asking for a written response, state when you expect to receive it. You should also relate any action that you will take and/or offer other important or relevant information such as an email address. If yours is a thank you letter, restate your thanks in this last paragraph.

5. Proofread your letter, and make sure that its *tone* is both <u>polite</u> and <u>respectful</u>. Proofread it for correct *spelling, capitalization, punctuation,* and *usage.*

6. Type your letter, if possible, and <u>make sure</u> that you *strictly follow* the correct <u>business letter form</u> found on the next page.

www.edudps.com

Heading:	Department of Health
	123 Main St.
	Anywhere, AL 12345-6789
Date:	January 2, 2003

FOUR SPACES

Inside Address:	Mr. Tom Johnson
	Taco Hut and Eatery
	The Ridgeway Mall
	321 First Street
	Somewhere, CA 09876-5432

DOUBLE SPACE

Salutation:	Dear Mr. Johnson:
(a colon <u>only</u>)	

DOUBLE SPACE

Body:	_____
	_____
	_____

DOUBLE SPACE

	_____
(Note: Do not	_____
indent para-	_____
graphs.)	_____
	_____

DOUBLE SPACE

Complimentary Closing:	Sincerely,
	(Signature here)

FOUR SPACES

	John Doe

DOUBLE SPACE

Initials-	JD: ag
Enclosures	Encl. Health Inspection Certificate
Copies:	cc: Frank Smith, Taco Hut and Eatery Area Manager

HOW TO TAKE NOTES

(From Reading or Written Material)

1. Skim the selection (this includes a book, article, or other literary work) first to gain understanding and meaning and to become familiar with the material.
2. Read the selection carefully. Highlight or underline any key words or phrases as you read. Look for the main ideas and necessary details. Usually the first and last lines of paragraphs are summary statements. In other words, these sentences usually contain main points or ideas.
3. Write down as notes the main points, key words, and phrases in concise form. Remember, do not elaborate when taking notes.

HOW TO WRITE AN OUTLINE

An outline is a list of the main and supporting ideas from a lecture or written material. Outlines are often used when taking notes from lectures or textbooks and for preparing essays, speeches, and research papers. After learning to write outlines, you may find that this is the easiest and most effective way to take notes.

The correct form of an outline is as follows: (Take particular note of where the indentions are and where Roman numerals, numbers, and letters are used.)

I. First main idea or Heading
    A. Subheading (supports first main idea)
        1. Detail (supports subheading A.)
        2. Detail (supports subheading A.)
    B. Subheading (supports first main idea)

II.   Second main idea or Heading
      A. Subheading (supports second main idea)
      B. Subheading (supports second main idea)
         1. Detail (supports subheading B.)
         2. Detail (supports subheading B.)

Follow these important points about outline form:

1. Outlines can be written in *sentences* or in *words or phrases*. Outlines written in sentences are called <u>sentence outlines</u>. Outlines written as words or phrases are called <u>topical outlines</u>. Mixing the two outline forms together is <u>not</u> acceptable. Choose one form over the other, and write in that form <u>only</u> during the complete outline. In other words, you cannot have some points written as sentences (sentence outline) and some points written as words or phrases (topical outline). Your outline must be either all sentences or all words or phrases.
2. Every entry in your outline must begin with a capital letter.
3. If you have a letter A in your outline, you <u>must</u> have a letter B. If you have a number 1, then you <u>must</u> have a number 2.

STEPS TO WRITING AN OUTLINE

⇒ *Main ideas* or *main topics* are the most important points an author makes and are listed as the headings in an outline.

⇒ *Subheadings* come under the main ideas and support, prove, or explain the main ideas and topics.

⇒ *Supporting details* are any facts that support, prove or explain the subheadings.

1. Decide whether you will use a sentence or topical outline form.
2. When reading, listening, or coming up with an outline for a writing assignment, make a list of the main and supporting ideas about your

subject. If you are listening to a lecture where you can follow the main and supporting ideas, write your outline in correct form as you listen. If you are reading material to be outlined, and the main and supporting ideas are clear, write them in your chosen outline form while reading.

3. After you finish listening to the lecture, reading your material, or jotting down ideas about your subject, arrange your main headings correctly. Roman numerals <u>must</u> be used with your main headings. Decide which points will be subheadings and which points will be supporting details, and group all of your points under the main headings correctly.

4. Write your final copy in correct form by making sure that you have followed all of the requirements.

Sample: Topical Outline

There are no punctuation marks at the ends of <u>topical</u> outline entries.

Good Manners

I.   Importance of
     A. Consideration of Other People
     B. Better Relationships With People

II.   Types
     A. Phone Manners
        1. Correct Greeting
        2. Taking Messages
     B. Greeting Manners
        1. Introduction
        2. Daily Courtesy
     C. Table Manners
        1. Talking

2. Chewing

3. Grabbing

Sample: **Sentence** Outline

There <u>are</u> punctuation marks at the ends of <u>sentence</u> outline entries.

Good Manners

I. Good Manners are important in life.
   A. Good manners demonstrate a consideration of others.
   B. Good manners help build better relationships with people.
II. There are several types of manners.
   A. Phone manners are important.
      1. You should greet people and state who is talking when you answer the phone.
      2. You should take a message when someone is not available.
   B. Greeting manners should be used daily.
      1. You should greet someone correctly and politely when you are introduced to them.
      2. You should courteously greet people each time you see them on a daily basis.
   C. Table manners benefit everyone.
      1. You should not talk with food in your mouth.
      2. You should chew with your mouth closed.
      3. You should not reach over others to grab an item.

HOW TO WRITE A SUMMARY

1. Read the selection that you are summarizing carefully so that you thoroughly understand it.

2. List the main points of the selection on paper. Write these as sentences, or simply jot down key words and phrases. Usually, the first and last sentences of paragraphs are summarizing sentences. Important details such as names, dates, times, and places should also be recorded.

3. Decide on and write down a topic sentence for your summary. This sentence must basically state the main idea of the selection – what the selection is trying to say.

4. Continue to write your summary by looking at the main points you have written on paper. Write in your own words, but <u>do</u> <u>not</u> add any of <u>your</u> <u>own</u> ideas. You are to restate the points of the selection that you have read. In restating, you must not change names, dates, times, and places. Never begin by saying, "This article or book was about…." Write just like the author did, but in your own words.

5. End with a concluding sentence. It should be a restatement (in different words) of your topic sentence.

6. Proofread your summary.

HOW TO WRITE A PERSUASIVE ESSAY

⇒ A persuasive essay is a written composition that tries to <u>convince</u> readers <u>to</u> <u>believe</u> the way that the author does about something.

Types of Persuasive Essays:

⇒ An editorial wherein you give your opinion about a current event or important topic and suggest a new course of action or solution to a problem.

⇒ An argumentative paper in which you are trying to convince your readers to accept your position about a subject.

⇒ A composition that focuses on something that you disagree with.

⇒ A literary analysis or book review.

1. Arrive at a topic. (Many times you will be assigned a topic relating to your study of history or literature.) Make sure that your topic can be truly argued (that it has at least two sides) and that it is specific and focused, not general and vague.

2. Write down all of your thoughts and knowledge about the subject.

3. Gather other details and facts about the subject by research, if necessary. You must *have enough facts to persuade* others.

4. Devise your thesis statement. In a persuasive essay, this is your opinion about the subject. This is the sentence that gives your essay direction and purpose and <u>can</u> be debated. It (a) <u>must</u> <u>be</u> related to the subject of your paper and (b) give the <u>reason</u> and <u>purpose</u> for the paper.

5. List the main points that prove or support your thesis statement or opinion. It will be helpful to write a brief topical or sentence outline to help organize your thoughts.

6. Write your introductory paragraph. It should start out with an "attention grabber". This can be an important quote, background information or specific fact(s) about your topic, a brief story, some form of humor, one or more questions about the topic or the definition of an important term. Introduce your subject and end your introductory paragraph with your thesis statement. This paragraph should be about five to seven sentences.

7. Write your supporting or body paragraphs. The body paragraphs are where you will prove and support your thesis statement. Write one paragraph for each point that supports your thesis statement. Each paragraph in the body must start with a topic sentence and each topic sentence must answer the question <u>why</u>? about your thesis statement in your introductory paragraph. Each paragraph must also end with a concluding sentence that restates your topic sentence. You must use specific facts and details to support your thesis statement. If you are writing about a piece of literature, you must use examples <u>from the literature</u> for support. Information in your paragraph must relate to your topic sentence and not stray from the topic. Use transition words to start each paragraph such as "First", "To start with", "Next", "Secondly", "Third", "Lastly", etc.

8. End your essay with a concluding paragraph that restates your thesis statement and sums up your main points. This paragraph must begin by restating the thesis statement. Then summarize your main points, and use another attention grabber to end the paragraph. You may use the same things covered above for attention grabbers, or you may end with a notable example of your argument. <u>Do not</u> introduce anything new in the concluding paragraph.

9. Proofread your essay for capitalization, punctuation, spelling, and grammar.

www.edudps.com

HOW TO WRITE AN EXPOSITORY ESSAY

⇒ An expository essay is a written composition that <u>informs</u> the reader about a meaningful subject.

Types of Expository Essays:

⇒ A written composition that describes how something works or how to do something.

⇒ A comparative paper wherein you examine the similarities and/or differences between two or among more than two subjects or ideas.

⇒ A composition where a problem and its solution are presented.

⇒ A descriptive paper about a person, place, or thing that is important to you.

⇒ A written description in which you give the details of a specific event or time in your life and what you learned from this experience.

⇒ A composition where you define or explain a word or term.

1. Choose a topic, or ask your teacher for a topic relating to a subject or piece of literature that you are studying. Narrow your subject down so that your topic is specific. Determine the focus of your writing. For example, if you are writing about drug abuse, what will your main focus be? – the effects of drug abuse or the cures of drug abuse. An expository essay <u>only</u> informs the reader about a meaningful or interesting subject. It does not argue a point or try to convince a reader of anything. See "Types of Expository Essays" above.

2. Write down all of the information that you know about the topic and do research for more details if necessary. To adequately inform your readers, you need information backed up by facts and/or statistics.

3. Form the thesis statement of your expository essay <u>by stating the focus</u> of your writing. This focus must express a specific feeling or take

a specific stand about the subject. For example, "The effects of drug abuse on an individual can damage his health for a lifetime."

4. After writing your thesis statement, arrange your ideas in a logical and organized manner by writing a sentence or topical outline.

5. Write your introductory paragraph and the rest of this expository essay, following the same guidelines in numbers 6-8 in "HOW TO WRITE A PERSUASIVE ESSAY". <u>Make</u> <u>sure</u> that you give specific details, examples, and quotations to support your thesis statement. The topic sentences of your paragraphs must prove and support your thesis statement. Also make sure that you use specific nouns and vivid adjectives, verbs, and adverbs – <u>especially</u> if you are writing a descriptive essay, which is a type of expository essay.

6. Proofread your essay for capitalization, punctuation, spelling, and grammar.

HOW TO WRITE A LITERARY CRITIQUE AND A BOOK REVIEW

Note: Numbers 1-5, 8 and 9 on the following pages apply to both literary critiques and book reviews. Number 6 applies only to book reviews. Number 7 applies only to literary critiques.

LITERARY CRITIQUE

⇒ **Literary critique:** an evaluation and judgment of a certain aspect or some aspects of a literary work such as a character, the plot, the theme, the setting, the imagery or style. Strengths and faults are analyzed, and then a judgment is made.

Any type of literary work can be critiqued such as a novel, biography, autobiography, short story, essay, article, poem, or play. Sometimes several literary works of an author are analyzed at the same time, or two authors are compared and analyzed.

BOOK REVIEW

⇒ **Book review:** a form of literary critique where a book is analyzed and <u>summarized</u> and its strengths and weaknesses are discussed. A final judgement is given about the book.

1. If you are given an assignment where you can choose the literary work or book, choose one that you are very familiar with and that you have strong feelings about or one that taught you something.

2. Skim the selection again if needed and/or take notes on the selection. What caught your attention the most? Write down the main parts of the selection. Next, write down all of your thoughts about the selection. List things you like about it and things that you don't like. If you are writing a critique and not a book review, you need to think of a part or parts of the literary work that you would like to analyze such as the theme, character, tone, or the plot.

3. Review your list from #2. Circle the points that you want to include in your critique or review.

4. Come up with your thesis statement for your paper. If you are writing a literary critique, your statement should tell the main point(s) that you will make in your paper regarding a certain aspect or aspects of the literary work. If you are writing a book review, this sentence will tell about one or more aspects of the book that made an impression on you. This can be something that you learned from the book or something others could learn from the book.

5. In your introduction, the first sentence should state the title, author, and theme(s) or subject(s) of the literary selection. In this sentence you should also state the type of literary form or book that you are analyzing or reviewing such as a poem, sonnet, novel, biography, etc. An example is: "*The Scarlet Letter*, a novel by Nathaniel Hawthorne, deals with the problem of sin that everyone must face." Next, use an "attention grabber" to arrest the attention of your readers. This can be a quotation from the selection, some background information about the selection or author or information about the setting (time and place) of the selection. If you are writing a literary critique, use a quote, if possible, and comment on its importance in relation to your thesis statement. The last sentence of your introductory paragraph will be your thesis statement that you wrote under #4.

6. If you are writing a book review (book report), follow these guidelines for writing the body paragraphs: (a) The body of your review should begin with a paragraph that summarizes the selection. This summary should include only the main points of the selection. See "HOW TO WRITE A SUMMARY" on pages 90-91. **Note:** If you are reviewing a fictional book or short story, write a summary of the plot (the events in the book). Introduce this by stating any conflict or problem in the book between or among its characters. Make sure that you tell how the conflict is resolved. (See "Writing A Short Story" in *WRITE WITH*

THE BEST – Vol. 1 on page 37 for a detailed explanation of the parts of a short story or other fictional work.) If you are reviewing a biography, summarize the main events of the person's life. If you are reviewing a nonfiction book or article, write a summary following the guidelines under "HOW TO WRITE A SUMMARY" in the "HOW TO WRITE GUIDE". If you are reviewing a poem, write a <u>brief</u> summary of the content of the poem. (b) The other paragraphs of the body should support the statement of opinion (i.e., the thesis statement) that you made in the introductory paragraph. Use details and quotations, when possible, in order to support your opinion. (The body should be two or more paragraphs long.)

7. When writing a literary critique, you are to use the body to support your thesis statement that you made in the introductory paragraph. Each paragraph in the body must begin with a topic sentence that supports your thesis statement. The rest of the paragraph <u>must</u> then <u>include</u> specific details or direct quotations <u>from</u> <u>the</u> <u>literary</u> <u>work</u>. You <u>must</u> <u>explain</u> *how* these details prove your point. (The body should be two or more paragraphs long.)

8. When writing your conclusion, begin by restating your opinion or thesis statement expressed in your introductory paragraph. Use different words in your restatement. If you are writing a book review, tell your opinion about the book – whether you like it or dislike it and whether you would recommend it to someone else. Give specific details about why you like it or dislike it, without introducing anything new. Include facts about the characters, setting, the action, the descriptive language of the writer or the dialogue. If you are writing a literary analysis, make sure that you leave your readers with a final, unforgettable thought about the literary work.

9. Proofread your literary analysis or book review carefully for punctuation, capitalization, usage, and grammar.

HOW TO WRITE A NEWSPAPER ARTICLE

1. A newspaper article is usually written to describe a specific event or person. Choose an event or person that you think is important and interesting enough to write about.

2. Write down everything that you know about this event or person, including the sights, sounds, smells, feelings, etc. that you remember from the event or any descriptions about the person. Also, write down any conversation that took place.

3. Refine or add to your descriptions covered under #2 by using specific nouns instead of generic ones and vivid or descriptive adjectives, verbs, and adverbs instead of dull or unimaginative ones.

4. Answer these six questions: Who?, What?, When?, Where?, Why?, and How? about your event or person.

5. Using the facts established under #'s 2 and 3, arrive at one main idea or focus that you want to convey when you write your article.

6. Come up with your first sentences for your article. Introduce your subject and main idea in an interesting way that will grab the attention of your readers.

7. Finish writing your article, incorporating the answers to the six questions asked under #4. Make sure that you have enough details to describe your event thoroughly, without being too wordy. Like a summary, a newspaper article must be concise and only give the most important details.

8. Conclude your article by summing up the main points that you are describing and restating your main idea or focus.

9. Arrive at a title for your article. Your title should state the main idea or focus of your writing. It should also be brief and should be "eye-catching", meaning that it must catch the reader's attention.

10. Proofread your entire article, making sure that all of the items covered under #'s 1-9 are clear.

HOW TO WRITE A SPEECH

1. Choose a topic and decide on your purpose for speaking. Are you going to give information, persuade someone of your viewpoint or opinion or show how to do something or how something works? If you are permitted to choose your own topic, you need to choose a subject that you are interested in, one that will really interest your audience, and one that you know a lot about or can learn a lot about easily. Your topic must be specific and not so broad that it will not be able to be adequately covered in a speech. You must think about your audience when you choose your topic. What is your audience interested in? What reasonable questions do they have? What would they really <u>like</u> to know? What do they <u>need</u> to know?

2. Collect all of the information that you need for your speech. If you are writing an informative speech or one that shows how to do something, you will need many details and facts. If you are writing a speech to persuade, you will need enough information and facts to support your argument. (**Note:** When giving your speech, you may also want to provide pictures, maps, charts, or objects to make your speech more interesting.)

3. Come up with a thesis statement that states the purpose of your speech. <u>Unlike</u> an essay or literary critique, a thesis statement for a speech will start by saying, "My purpose is to (persuade, inform, explain, demonstrate)..."

4. Organize all of your information from #2 into an outline. You should write a sentence outline. This outline is important because when you give the speech, you may use it as your notes. Topical outlines do not have the detail of sentence outlines.

5. Write the introduction by starting with an "attention grabber". (See "HOW TO WRITE A PERSUASIVE ESSAY" for examples of attention grabbers.) After the attention grabber, you should introduce your

topic – tell a little about it, and then end your first paragraph with your thesis statement from #3.

6. Write the body paragraphs by beginning with a topic sentence that supports your thesis statement.

7. You must have one paragraph for *each* main point that you are making. Your points <u>must</u> relate to your thesis statement.

8. Each paragraph must start with a topic sentence and end with a concluding sentence.

9. Use transition words at the start of each paragraph to help your points flow together.

10. Write your conclusion by starting with another short "attention grabber". You may use an interesting fact or story as your attention grabber here. The conclusion should restate all of your <u>most</u> important points. Once again, you should let your audience know *why* the topic you chose is important and *whether* they should take any action concerning what you have said.

11. Proofread your speech for errors, and read it out loud to make sure it is effective.

HOW TO WRITE A DRAMATIC MONOLOGUE

1. Choose a character from a book that you have read or a person that you have studied who was involved in a dramatic event or situation.

2. Decide on a conflict or situation involving this character or person that you can base a dramatic monologue upon. This conflict or situation must be one that is significant. There must be facts about your character, the situation, and/or other people involved that you will reveal through your character's monologue.

3. Write down everything that you can think of about the character or person that you have chosen to speak your monologue. Write descriptive words and actions to <u>describe</u> <u>this</u> <u>individual</u>. Use specific nouns to describe him or her. Decide which specific things about the character's personality you will bring out in the dramatic monologue.

4. Decide on the main purpose or theme that you will convey through the monologue.

5. Write down some specific nouns and vivid adjectives, verbs, and adverbs that you will use to make the monologue "come alive" for your readers.

6. Write your monologue, opening with something that will grab the attention of your audience.

7. In the monologue, make sure that you <u>reveal</u> or *bring out* certain characteristics, motives, emotions, facts, etc. about your character, the other people involved and/or the dramatic situation itself.

8. Make sure that your character speaks somewhat at length <u>and</u> without interruption throughout his conversation – the monologue.

9. End the dramatic monologue with a lasting statement – something your audience will not forget.

10. Proofread your monologue.

www.edudps.com

GRADING CRITERIA

Parents and Teachers,

Some of you will choose to issue numerical grades for each writing assignment. To aid you in this, the proofreading checklists for each genre include the number of points that each item on the checklist should count for grading purposes. Make a copy of each checklist and use it to evaluate your student's writing. Place this with the completed work in your student's portfolio.

Important Proofreading Note: Each genre in Vol. 2 requires that two (2) proofreading checklists should be completed by the student: 1) the checklist for the specific genre such as "Proofreading Checklist For A Speech" and 2) the "GENERAL PURPOSE PROOFREADING CHECKLIST" on page 114.

PROOFREADING CHECKLIST FOR POETRY IN FREE VERSE

Put a (√) if present and an (×) if not present.

Grading Criteria: Each item counts 11.11 points.

- ____ There is a clear theme or message in the poem.
- ____ The tone of the poem is clear.
- ____ A specific memory, feeling, belief, opinion, experience, object or person is described.
- ____ There are clear word pictures or imagery in the poem.
- ____ Specific nouns and descriptive verbs, adverbs, and adjectives are present.
- ____ Figurative language and poetic devices have been used.
- ____ When the poem is read aloud, you can hear rhythm without rhyme.
- ____ The conclusion relates a special or exciting detail.
- ____ Spelling, grammar, punctuation and capitalization are correct. (Complete the proofreading checklist on page 114.)

PROOFREADING CHECKLIST FOR
A BUSINESS LETTER

Put a (√) if present and an (×) if not present.
Grading Criteria: Each item counts 14.28 points.

- ____ The purpose of the letter is clear.
- ____ The introductory paragraph states the purpose and includes an introduction of the writer.
- ____ The middle paragraph(s) present(s) the detailed information needed to communicate the purpose clearly, convincingly, and effectively.
- ____ The concluding paragraph includes any action expected from the recipient.
- ____ The concluding paragraph expresses thanks to the recipient of the letter.
- ____ The letter is in correct business letter form – see page 86.
- ____ There is correct spelling, punctuation, capitalization, and grammar. (Complete the proofreading checklist on page 114.)

PROOFREADING CHECKLIST
FOR AN OUTLINE

Put a (√) if present and an (×) if not present.
Grading Criteria: Each item counts 12.5 points.

- ____ The outline is <u>clearly</u> a topical or sentence outline. (There is no mixture of the two outline types.)
- ____ Topical outlines do <u>not</u> have ending punctuation. Sentence outlines <u>have</u> ending punctuation.
- ____ All headings (or main ideas) have Roman numerals.
- ____ Subheadings come under main headings or ideas, have capital letters (A., B., etc.), and <u>support</u> the main ideas.
- ____ If subheadings have details, they <u>support</u> the subheadings and are numbered (1., 2., 3., etc.).
- ____ <u>Each</u> entry in the outline begins with a capital letter.
- ____ If the outline has a letter A. entry, there is also a letter B. entry.
- ____ If the outline has a number 1 entry, there is also a number 2 entry.

PROOFREADING CHECKLIST
FOR A SUMMARY

Put a (√) if present and an (×) if not present.
Grading Criteria: Each item counts 14.28 points.

- ____ The summary begins with a topic sentence that states the main idea(s) of the selection.
- ____ The body sentences of the summary state <u>only</u> the most important points of the selection.
- ____ Important names, dates, times, and places are listed.
- ____ The summary is written in your own words and not in the exact words of the author of the selection.
- ____ No new ideas are added. (You have simply restated the ideas of the author.)
- ____ The summary ends with a concluding sentence that re-states the topic sentence in different words.
- ____ There is correct capitalization, punctuation, spelling, and usage. (Complete the proofreading checklist on page 114.)

www.edudps.com

PROOFREADING CHECKLIST
FOR ESSAYS – PERSUASIVE AND EXPOSITORY

Put a (√) if present and an (×) if not present.

Grading Criteria: For a persuasive essay, each item counts 10 points. For an expository essay, each item counts 10 points.

- ____ The topic of the essay is specific and focused.

- ____ There is an "attention grabber" at the beginning of the first paragraph – the introductory paragraph.

- ____ The thesis statement is the last sentence of the first paragraph <u>and</u> is clear.

- ____ Each body paragraph has an adequate topic sentence that supports the thesis statement.

- ____ Each body paragraph discusses only one idea.

- ____ The body paragraphs begin with transition words such as "First", "Second", "Lastly", etc.

- ____ Each body paragraph ends with a concluding sentence which restates the topic sentence.

- ____ If it is a persuasive essay, the body paragraphs contain adequate information <u>to</u> <u>prove</u> the thesis statement and argue the main points realistically and effectively.

- ____ If it is an expository essay, the body paragraphs contain enough facts, examples, and details <u>to</u> <u>thoroughly</u> <u>explain</u> the thesis statement.

- ____ The concluding paragraph rephrases the thesis statement, sums up the main points, and ends with an attention grabber – a lasting and final thought that the readers cannot easily forget.

- ____ There is correct spelling, punctuation, capitalization, and grammar. (Complete the proofreading checklist on page 114.)

PROOFREADING CHECKLIST
FOR A LITERARY CRITIQUE

Put a (√) if present and an (×) if not present.
Grading Criteria: Each item counts 14.28 points.

- ____ The first sentence of the introductory paragraph states the title, author, type of genre and theme of the literary selection.
- ____ The introductory paragraph includes an "attention grabber".
- ____ The thesis statement is the last sentence of the introductory paragraph and includes information about *an aspect* or *aspects* of the literary work that you are critiquing.
- ____ The body paragraphs fully support the thesis statement by providing specific details or direct quotations <u>from the literary work</u>.
- ____ The concluding paragraph restates the thesis statement in different words.
- ____ The concluding paragraph includes a final, unforgettable thought about the literary work.
- ____ Punctuation, capitalization, grammar, and spelling are correct. (Complete the proofreading checklist on page 114.)

PROOFREADING CHECKLIST
FOR A BOOK REVIEW

Put a (√) if present and an (×) if not present.
Grading Criteria: Each item counts 12.5 points.

- ____ The introductory paragraph begins by stating the title, author, theme or subject and the type of book that you are reviewing.

- ____ The introductory paragraph contains an "attention grabber" such as a quote, background information, or other interesting information.

- ____ The thesis statement is the last statement of the introductory paragraph and tells about one part of the book such as a moral concept that impressed you.

- ____ The body of the book review begins with a summary paragraph about the book.

- ____ The remaining body paragraphs use details and quotations to support your thesis statement.

- ____ The conclusion begins by restating the thesis statement in different words.

- ____ The conclusion states your opinion about the book, validated by specific details and whether you do or do not recommend it to someone else.

- ____ Punctuation, capitalization, grammar, and spelling are correct. (Complete the proofreading checklist on page 114.)

PROOFREADING CHECKLIST
FOR A NEWSPAPER ARTICLE

Put a (√) if present and an (×) if not present.
Grading Criteria: Each item counts 10 points.

- ____ The event (or person) is very clearly described.
- ____ The main idea or focus of the article is clear.
- ____ The first sentences of the article "grab" the attention of the reader.
- ____ The body of the article brings the main points of the article together in a supportive way.
- ____ The six questions (i.e., Who?, What?, When? Where?, Why?, and How?) are clearly answered about the event or person.
- ____ Specific nouns and descriptive adjectives, verbs, and adverbs have been used throughout.
- ____ The words used in the article are concise, and only the most important details are given.
- ____ The conclusion sums up the main points of the article and restates its main idea or focus.
- ____ The title of the article states the main idea or focus of the article and is concise and "catchy".
- ____ Spelling, grammar, capitalization, and punctuation are correct. (Complete the proofreading checklist on page 114.)

PROOFREADING CHECKLIST
FOR A SPEECH

Put a (√) if present and an (×) if not present.
Grading Criteria: Each item counts 11.11 points.

- ____ The topic and the importance of the topic are clear.
- ____ The introductory paragraph of the speech has an "attention grabber".
- ____ The introductory paragraph of the speech includes a thesis statement at the end that <u>explicitly</u> states the purpose of the speech – to persuade, inform, or demonstrate.
- ____ The body paragraphs of the speech support or prove the thesis statement.
- ____ There is one body paragraph for each main point.
- ____ Each body paragraph begins with a topic sentence and ends with a concluding sentence.
- ____ There are transition words at the beginning of the body paragraphs such as "First", "Next", "Last", etc.
- ____ The conclusion of the speech sums up the main points, tells why they are important, leaves the audience with a lasting thought, and states any action that should be taken.
- ____ Punctuation, capitalization, grammar, and spelling are correct. (Complete the proofreading checklist on page 114.)

PROOFREADING CHECKLIST
FOR A DRAMATIC MONOLOGUE

Put a (√) if present and an (×) if not present.
Grading Criteria: Each item counts 10 points.

- ____ The character chosen was involved in a significant conflict or problem – a dramatic event.
- ____ The dramatic monologue <u>reveals</u> special characteristics, motives, emotions, intrigues, events, facts, etc. that arise from the dramatic event.
- ____ The purpose or theme of the monologue is clear.
- ____ The dramatic monologue is relatively long and the character giving it <u>is</u> <u>not</u> interrupted by another character during his talk.
- ____ The character's personality is clearly portrayed.
- ____ There are enough specific nouns and descriptive adjectives, verbs, and adverbs to vividly portray the <u>character</u>.
- ____ Some figurative language has been used.
- ____ The opening of the monologue has an "attention grabber".
- ____ The conclusion leaves the readers with a lasting memory.
- ____ There is correct capitalization, punctuation, spelling, and usage. (Complete the proofreading checklist on page 114.)

www.edudps.com

GENERAL PURPOSE PROOFREADING CHECKLIST

Note: Some of these will not apply to all genres such as poetry, a business letter, etc.

- ____ Each paragraph is indented.
- ____ Each paragraph has at least 5 sentences.
- ____ All sentences begin with a capital letter.
- ____ All sentences end with a punctuation mark.
- ____ Each paragraph has a good <u>beginning</u> or <u>topic</u> sentence.
- ____ Each paragraph has a good <u>ending</u> or <u>concluding</u> sentence.
- ____ All sentences relate to the topic.
- ____ Most verbs, adverbs, and adjectives are vivid or descriptive.
- ____ Some nouns are specific rather than generic. For example, "fellow" is used instead of "man".
- ____ All sentences are complete – there are no run-on sentences or fragments.
- ____ All important words (proper nouns) have capital letters.
- ____ The same words are not used too often. For example, words such as "then" or "said".
- ____ The sentences have different lengths. Not all are very short and not all are very long.
- ____ Different kinds of sentences are included – compound, complex, etc.
- ____ Each subject agrees with its verb. For example, improper subject-verb agreement would be: "The dogs barks".
- ____ The same verb tense is used throughout the paper. For example, if you start a story in past tense (what has happened in the past), you must continue with this tense throughout the story.

www.edudps.com

SELECT ANSWER KEY TO CITED LITERARY PASSAGES

The select answer key is divided between sentence answers, phrase answers, and parts of speech answers.

Parts of Speech Note: Not <u>all</u> nouns, verbs, adjectives, and adverbs in each literary passage are listed in this answer key – only some specific nouns and the most descriptive verbs, adjectives, and adverbs that the author uses to create word pictures for the readers.

Adjectives in the form of "of ___" are prepositional phrases used as adjectives.

- All parts of speech entries in the answer key are placed in alphabetical order under each particular part of speech.
- We have not changed the spelling of the parts of speech listed. We have reproduced the spelling as rendered by each author.

Remember that younger and inexperienced students should not be expected to find every example.

UNIT 1

Day 1

The train is compared to an animal, a person, Boanerges, and a star.

No, this poem, like all free verse, does not rhyme.

Day 2

UNIT 1 – PARTS OF SPEECH
"The Railway Train"

Specific Nouns (circle)	Descriptive Verbs (green)	Descriptive Adjectives (red)
Boanerges	chase	docile

(circle)	(green)	(red)
pile	complaining	hooting
quarry	crawl	horrid
shanties	feed	omnipotent
stanza	fit	prodigious
star	lap	punctual
tanks	lick	supercilious
	neigh	
	pare	
	peer	
	step	
	stop	

Day 4

Answers to questions:

1. lapping, licking, and feeding
2. crawling, complaining, chasing
3. "neigh like Boanerges" and "punctual as a star"
4. "**h**orrid, **h**ooting stanza"
5. Yes
6. The calm and assured stopping of the train at its shelter
7. lighthearted and playful
8. A horse

UNIT 4

Day 2

- A persuasive essay tries to <u>convince</u> the readers <u>to believe</u> the author's viewpoint(s).
- Thesis statement: "I challenge the warmest advocate for reconciliation, to shew, a single advantage that this continent can reap, by being connected with Great Britain."
- Mr. Paine grabs the attention of his readers by presenting a challenge and then repeating himself. He also gives specific facts up front about the financial concerns of his readers.

Day 3

- To support his thesis statement, Mr. Paine shows the <u>disadvantages</u> of reconciliation with Great Britain. The main points of Mr. Paine's arguments are:
  1. Reconciliation will "set us at variance with" other nations.
  2. If war breaks out between England and another country, the trade of America will be ruined.
  3. The distance that God made between England and America shows that we should not reconcile.
  4. England's authoritative government over America must eventually come to an end for the sake of our children.
  5. We cannot reconcile with a power that has brought "fire and sword" into our land.
- Mr. Paine leaves his readers with a lasting and final thought by addressing his audience in urgency and giving examples of other continents that have "expelled" freedom and are therefore, "overrun with oppression". He ends by personifying freedom to make his point.

Day 12

- An expository essay <u>informs</u> the readers about a meaningful subject.
- The thesis statement is: "Studies serve for delight, for ornament, and for ability."
- He is explaining the merits of the different kinds of studies.
- He is doing <u>all</u> four of these things.

UNIT 5

Day 2

- Hawthorne's strengths:
    1. contains best American prose so far
    2. a pure style
    3. effective tone
    4. remarkable originality within his themes in the tales
- Hawthorne's weaknesses:
    1. the title of his book
    2. not enough diversity in the character of his themes

Day 3

- Mr. Poe analyzes Hawthorne's title, style, tone, themes, and "originality of incident and reflection".

Day 4

- Attention grabber: "We have always regarded the *Tale* (using this word in its popular acceptation) as affording the best prose opportunity for display of the highest talent. It has peculiar advantages which the novel does not admit. It is, of course, a far finer field than the essay."

- **Special note:** Like many of the early writers, Mr. Poe does not adhere to all of our modern rules of essay writing. Therefore, he does not include a thesis statement. *Include this objective under Day 4: Write an appropriate thesis statement for Poe's literary critique. Return to page 47.

Day 12

- Mr. Howells focuses mainly on the realistic character of Tom Sawyer and the accurate portrayal of life in the Southwest (the setting).
- Yes, he covers them thoroughly.
- He thoroughly covers these elements in the book by:

What?

- He describes Tom's specific character traits.
- He describes Tom's dreams and adventures.
- He gives us a full glimpse of the town Tom lives in by describing the characters of the town.

How?

- Mr. Howells uses excellent <u>descriptive</u> words to bring his characters to life for his readers.

Day 13

- Mr. Howells' attention grabber is: "Mr. Clemens has taken the boy of the Southwest for the hero of his new book, and has presented him with a fidelity to circumstance which loses no charm by being realistic in the highest degree, and which gives incomparably the best picture of life in that region as yet known to fiction."
- Yes, Mr. Howells does a superb job of summarizing the plot of the book in his description of some of Tom's adventures.
- Yes, Mr. Howells gives us his opinion of the book in the last line of the review, as well as throughout the review.

- He definitely thinks that Mr. Twain does an excellent job in *The Adventures of Tom Sawyer*.

UNIT 6

Day 1

PARTS OF SPEECH

"Would Treat 'Em Rough'"

Please note: I have listed only the most vivid. Just make sure that you marked some of these.

Specific Nouns (circle)	Descriptive Verbs (green)	Descriptive Adjectives (red)	Descriptive Adverbs (blue)
action	admitted	double lens	flashily
applicants	bawled	dressed	steadily
danger	bolted	gray haired	
exodus	crowded	mechanical	
glasses	moistening	quick	
mechanic	peeping	red faced	
perspiration	slipped	slight	
promotion	voiced	stout	
qualifications			
service			
slogan			

Day 2

- He is describing enlisting for World War I.
- Who? several men (some specifically described such as a stout man, a mechanic, a high school boy, an attorney)
- What? an army recruiting event

- When? 7:45 A.M., April 18, 1918
- Where? Twelfth Street and Grand Avenue
- Why? they came for "action" with the "tankers" in World War I.
- How? All are willing at first. Later, some leave for various reasons, but others remain steadfast and are recruited by Lieutenant Cooter.

Day 3

- Mr. Hemingway is reporting about the bravery of some men who apply for the army because they want to see action.
- He gets his main idea across by describing the characteristics, attributes, actions, and conversations of the different men who have come to enlist in the army.
- Mr. Hemingway's attention grabber is the first statement of the stout man: "I'm the treat 'em rough man," he bawled. "That cat in the poster has nothing on me. Where do you join the tankers?"
- Yes, his attention grabber appears within the first sentences of his article.
- Yes, to all three parts of the question.

UNIT 7

Day 3

- Cicero has written his speech to <u>persuade</u> his audience to pardon Gaius Rabirius who is accused of murder and to uphold the safety of the republic.
- **Red:** Cicero's purpose is told in the <u>second</u> sentence, unlike our rules for speech writing, which place the thesis statement at the end of the paragraph. Thesis statement: "For the ancientness of my friendship with him, and the dignity of the man, and a regard for humanity, and the uninterrupted practice of my life, have instigated me to defend

Gaius Rabirius; and also my duty as consul, the safety of the republic, and also that of each individual citizen in it as entrusted to me, compel me to do so with the greatest zeal."

- **Blue:** Cicero's "attention grabber" is found in the first sentence, in which he also declares that it is a departure from his custom to give reasons why he defends anyone – which he does give in this defense. Attention grabber: "Although, O Romans, it is not my custom at the beginning of a speech to give any reason why I am defending each particular defendant, because I have always considered that the mere fact of the danger of any citizen was quite sufficient reason for my considering myself connected with him, still, in this instance, when I come forward to defend the life, and character, and all the fortunes of Gaius Rabirius, I think I ought to give reasons for my undertaking this duty; because the very same reasons which have appeared to me as most adequate to prompt me to undertake his defense, ought also to appear to you sufficient to induce you to acquit him." Cicero also states up front that these reasons in themselves should "induce (the citizens) to acquit him". Also take note of the fact that Cicero's attention grabber is just where we would expect to find it in a modern speech – at the beginning of the speech.

Day 4

- Cicero persuades his audience by:
  1. telling of the character of Rabirius
  2. telling of his own duties to uphold justice
  3. telling the <u>real</u> <u>reason</u> why Rabirius is standing trial
  4. naming the virtues of the Romans who make up his audience, which will lead them to the proper action
  5. telling them that their attention and decision in this matter is of the <u>utmost</u> importance for the republic

6. urging his audience to realize why Rabirius did what he did and to pardon him
7. entreating the Romans to consider his argument and reject the accusation of murder and in this way to preserve the republic

- Cicero's concluding attention grabber is "I pray that this day may have dawned for the salvation of this man, and for the welfare of the republic." If you also chose his statement about the Roman's power coming near that of their gods, you are also correct. Both of these statements are attention grabbers.
- Yes, his final paragraph does all of those things.

UNIT 8

Day 1

- Shakespeare's main focus is the <u>true</u> character of Caesar opposed to Brutus' obvious opinion of Caesar.
- The occasion of the monologue is the aftermath of the assassination of Julius Caesar.
  Antony is speaking over Caesar's corpse at his funeral.

Day 2

- Playwrights include dramatic monologues in plays to (1) reveal important things about the character speaking (2) reveal important things about other characters (3) reveal secrets, motives, facts, and intrigues related to the plot, not known about or made known by the other characters. Return to page 74.

- Shakespeare depicts Mark Antony as a grieving man who deeply loves his deceased friend, Caesar, and who questions the motives of his assassins.

- Shakespeare wants his audience to know that what Brutus has done is highly questionable.
- He wants his audience to know that Caesar was not as ambitious as Brutus depicted him as being. He also wants them to know that the opposite was actually the case.
- Two examples of personification are:
  1. judgment fleeing
  2. Antony's heart departing and coming back

Day 3

PARTS OF SPEECH
Julius Caesar

Specific Nouns (circle)	Descriptive Verbs (green)	Descriptive Adjectives (red)
beasts	answer'd	ambitious
captives	cried	brutish
cause	fled	faithful
evil	interred	grievous
fault	lend	honourable
good	mourn	just
judgment	wept	noble
poor		sterner
		thrice

1. Mark Antony repeats the word "honourable" so often to show the audience that Brutus' character is really the one in question and probably not "honourable" at all.

2. He is attacking the cause of Caesar's assassination and thereby calling its motives and objectives into question.
3. Shakespeare gains the attention of his audience by the statements made in his opening two sentences, the first of which has become very famous.
4. The conflict is built around the validity and results of the very assassination of Julius Caesar.
5. Shakespeare ends the monologue by using figurative language (personification) to demonstrate the degree and intensity of Mark Antony's grief.

SELECT LITERARY PASSAGES

BUSINESS LETTER By Helen Keller

March 20, 1891

To Mr. George R. Krehl
Institution for the Blind
South Boston, Mass.

My Dear Friend, Mr. Krehl:

I have just heard, through Mr. Wade, of your kind offer to buy me a gentle dog, and I want to thank you for the kind thought. It makes me very happy indeed to know that I have such dear friends in other lands. It makes me think that all people are good and loving. I have read that the English and Americans are cousins; but I am sure it would be much truer to say that we are brothers and sisters. My friends have told me about your great and magnificent city, and I have read a great deal that wise Englishmen have written. I have begun to read "Enoch Arden," and I know several of the great poet's poems by heart. I am eager to cross the ocean, for I want to see my English friends and their good and wise queen. Once the Earl of Meath came to see me, and he told me that the queen was much beloved by her people, because of her gentleness and wisdom. Some day you will be surprised to see a little strange girl coming into your office; but when you know it is the little girl who loves dogs and all other animals, you will laugh, and I hope you will give her a kiss, just as Mr. Wade does. He has another dog for me, and he thinks she will be as brave and faithful as my beautiful Lioness. And now I want to tell you what the dog lovers in America are going to do. They are going to send me some money for a poor little deaf and dumb and blind child. His name is Tommy, and he is five years old. His parents are too poor to pay to have the little fellow sent to school; so, instead of giving me a dog, the gentlemen are going to help make Tommy's life as bright and joyous as mine. Is it not a beautiful plan? Education will bring light and music into Tommy's soul, and then he cannot help being happy.

From your loving little friend,
HELEN A. KELLER.

LITERARY CRITIQUE of CHAUCER by John Dryden (1631-1700)

In the first place, as he is the Father of English Poetry, so I hold him in the same Degree of Veneration as the Grecians held Homer, or the Romans Virgil: He is a perpetual Fountain of good Sense; learn'd in all Sciences; and, therefore speaks properly on all Subjects: As he knew what to say, so he knows also when to leave off; a Continence which is practis'd by few Writers, and scarcely by any of the Ancients, excepting Virgil and Horace.

Chaucer follow'd Nature every where, but was never so bold to go beyond her: And there is a great Difference of being *Poeta* and *nimis Poeta*, if we may believe Catullus, as much as betwixt a modest Behaviour and Affectation. The Verse of Chaucer, I confess, is not Harmonious to us; but 'tis like the Eloquence of one whom Tacitus commends, it was *auribus istius temporis accommodate*: They who liv'd with him, and some time after him, thought it Musical; and it continues so even in our Judgment, if compar'd with the Numbers of Lidgate and Gower, his Contemporaries: There is the rude Sweetness of a Scotch Tune in it, which is natural and pleasing, though not perfect.

'Tis true, I cannot go so far as he who publish'd the last Edition of him; for he would make us believe the Fault is in our Ears, and that there were really Ten Syllables in a Verse where we find but Nine: But this Opinion is not worth confuting; 'tis so gross and obvious an Errour, that common Sense (which is a Rule in everything but Matters of Faith and Revelation) must convince the Reader, that Equality of Numbers, in every Verse which we call Heroick, was either not known, or not always practis'd, in Chaucer's Age. It were an easie Matter to produce some thousands of his Verses, which are lame for want of half a Foot, and sometimes a whole one, and which no Pronunciation can make otherwise. We can only say, that he liv'd in the Infancy of our Poetry, and that nothing is brought to Perfection at the first. We must be Children before we grow Men. There was an Ennius, and in process of Time a Lucilius, and a Lucretius, before Virgil and Horace; even after Chaucer there was a Spencer, a Harrington, a Fairfax, before Waller and Denham were in being: And our Numbers were in their Nonage till these last appeared.

He must have been a Man of a most wonderful comprehensive Nature, because, as it has been truly observ'd of him, he has taken into the Compass of his Canterbury Tales the various Manners and Humours (as we now call them) of the whole English Nation, in his Age. Not a single Character has escap'd him. All his Pilgrims are severally distinguished from each other; and not only in their Inclinations, but in their very Phisiognomies and Persons. Baptista Porta could not have describ'd their

Natures better, than by the Marks which the Poet gives them. The Matter and Manner of their Tales, and of their Telling, are so suited to their different Educations, Humours, and Callings, that each of them would be improper in any other Mouth. Even the grave and serious Characters are distinguished by their several sorts of Gravity: Their Discourses are such as belong to their Age, their Calling, and their Breeding; such as are becoming of them, and of them only. Some of his Persons are Vicious, and some Vertuous; some are unlearn'd, or (as Chaucer calls them) Lewd, and some are Learn'd. Even the Ribaldry of the Low Characters is different: the Reeve, the Miller, and the Cook, are several Men, and are distinguished from each other, as much as the mincing Lady-Prioress, and the broad-speaking, gap-tooth'd wife of Bathe.

But enough of this: There is such a Variety of Game springing up before me, that I am distracted in my Choice, and know not which to follow. 'Tis sufficient to say according to the Proverb, that here is God's Plenty.

BOOK REVIEW by Henry Wadsworth Longfellow (1837)
of Nathaniel Hawthorne's *Twice-Told Tales*

When a new star rises in the heavens, people gaze after it for a season with the naked eye, and with such telescopes as they may find. In the stream of thought, which flows so peacefully deep and clear, through the pages of this book, we see the bright reflection of a spiritual star, after which men will be fain to gaze "with the naked eye, and with the spy-glasses of criticism." This star is but newly risen; and ere long the observations of numerous star-gazers, perched up on arm-chairs and editors' tables, will inform the world of its magnitude and its place in the heaven of poetry, whether it be in the paw of the Great Bear, or on the forehead of Pegasus, or on the strings of the Lyre, or in the wing of the Eagle. Our own observations are as follows.

To this little work we would say, "Live ever, sweet, sweet book." It comes from the hand of a man of genius. Every thing about it has the freshness of morning and of May. These flowers and green leaves of poetry have not the dust of the highway upon them. They have been gathered fresh from the secret places of a peaceful and gentle heart. There flow deep waters, silent, calm, and cool; and the green trees look into them, and "God's blue heaven." The book, though in prose, is written nevertheless by a poet. He looks upon all things in the spirit of love, and with lively sympathies; for to him external form is but the representation of internal being, all things having a life, an end and aim. The true poet is a friendly man. He takes to his arms even cold and inanimate things, and rejoices in his heart, as did St. Bernard of old, when he kissed his Bride of Snow. To his eye all things are beautiful and holy; all are objects of feeling and of song, from the great hierarchy of the silent, saint-like stars that rule the night, down to the little flowers which are "stars in the firmament of the earth."

There are some honest people into whose hearts "Nature cannot find the way." They have no imagination by which to invest the ruder forms of earthly things with poetry. They are like Wordsworth's Peter Bell;

"A primrose by a river's brim,
A yellow primrose was to him,
And it was nothing more."

But it is one of the high attributes of the poetic mind, to feel a universal sympathy with Nature, both in the material world and in the soul of man. It identifies itself likewise with every object of its sympathy, giving it new sensation and poetic life, whatever that object may be, whether man, bird, beast, flower, or star. As to the pure mind all things are pure, so to the poetic mind all things are poetical. To such souls no age and no country can be utterly dull and prosaic. They make unto themselves their age and country; dwelling in the universal mind of man, and in the universal forms of things. Of such is the author of this book.

The Twice-Told Tales are so called, we presume, from having been first published in various annuals and magazines, and now collected together, and told a second time in a volume by themselves. And a very delightful volume do they make; one of those, which excite in you a feeling of personal interest for the author, A calm, thoughtful face seems to be looking at you from every page; with now a pleasant smile, and now a shade of sadness stealing over its features. Sometimes, though not often, it glares wildly at you, with a strange and painful expression, as, in the German romance, the bronze knocker of the Archivarius Lindhorst makes up faces at the Student Anselmus.

One of the most prominent characteristics of these tales is, that they are national in their character. The author has wisely chosen his tales among the traditions of New England; the dusty legends of "the good Old Colony times, when we lived under a king." This is the right material for story. It seems as natural to make tales out of old tumble-down traditions, as canes and snuff-boxes out of old steeples, or trees planted by great men. The puritanical times begin to look romantic in the distance. Truly, many quaint and quiet customs, many comic scenes and strange adventures, many wild and wondrous things, fit for humorous tale and soft, pathetic story, lie all about us here in New England.

Another characteristic of this writer is the exceeding beauty of his style. It is as clear as running waters are. Indeed he uses words as mere stepping-stones, upon which, with a free and youthful bound, his spirit crosses and recrosses the bright and rushing stream of thought. Some writers of the present day have introduced a kind of Gothic architecture into their style. All is fantastic, vast, and wondrous in the outward form, and within is mysterious twilight, and the swelling sound of an organ, and a voice chanting hymns in Latin, which need a translation for many of the crowd. To this we do not object. Let the priest chant in what language he will, so long as he understands his own mass-book. But if he wishes the world to listen and be edified, he will do well to choose a language that is generally understood.

Consider the beautiful and simple style of the book before us, its vein of pleasant philosophy, and the quiet humor, which is to the face of a book what a smile is to the face of man. In speaking in terms of such high praise as we have done, we have given utterance not alone to our own feelings, but we trust to those of all gentle readers of the Twice-Told Tales. Like children we say, "Tell us more."

BOOK REVIEW by W. D. Howells
of Mark Twain's *A Connecticut Yankee in King Arthur's Court*
Harper's Magazine – January 1890

Mr. Clemens, we call him, rather than Mark Twain, because we feel that in this book our arch-humorist imparts more of his personal quality than in anything else he has done. Here he is to the full the humorist, as we know him; but he is very much more, and his strong, indignant, often infuriate hate of injustice, and his love of equality, burn hot through the manifold adventures and experiences of the tale. What he thought about prescriptive right and wrong, we had partly learned in *The Prince and the Pauper* and in *Huckleberry Finn*, but it is this last book which gives his whole mind. The elastic scheme of the romance allows it to play freely back and forward between the sixth century and the nineteenth century; and often while it is working the reader up to a blasting contempt of monarchy and aristocracy in King Arthur's time, the dates are magically shifted under him, and he is confronted with exactly the same principles in Queen Victoria's time. The delicious satire, the marvelous wit, the wild, free, fantastic humor are the colors of the tapestry, while the texture is a humanity that lives in every fibre. At every moment the scene amuses, but it is all the time an object-lesson in democracy. It makes us glad of our republic and our epoch; but it does not flatter us into a fond content with them; there are passages in which we see that the noble of Arthur's day who fattened on the blood and sweat of his bondmen, is one in essence with the capitalist of Mr. Harrison's day who grows rich on the labor of his underpaid wage-men....

Mr. Clemens's glimpses of monastic life in Arthur's realm are true enough; and if they are not the whole truth of the matter, one may easily get it in some such book as Mr. Brace's *Gesta Christi,* where the full light of history is thrown upon the transformation of the world, if not the Church, under the influence of Christianity. In the mean time, if any one feels that the justice done the churchmen of King Arthur's time is too much of one kind, let him turn to that heart-breaking scene where the brave monk stands with the mother and her babe on the scaffold, and execrates the hideous law which puts her to death for stealing enough to keep her from starving. It is one of many passages in the story where our civilization of today sees itself mirrored in the cruel barbarism of the past, the same in principle and only softened in custom. With shocks of consciousness, one recognizes in such episodes that the laws are still made for the few against the many, and that the preservation of things, not men, is still the ideal of legislation. But we do not wish to leave the reader with the notion that Mr. Clemens's work is otherwise than obliquely serious. Upon the face of it you have a story no more openly didactic than *Don Quixote,* which we found ourselves more than once thinking of as we read, though always with a sense of the kindlier and truer heart of our time. Never once, we believe, has Mark Twain been funny at the cost of the weak, the unfriended, the helpless; and this is rather more than you can say of Cid Hamet ben Engeli. But the two writers are of the same humorous largeness; and when the Connecticut man rides out at dawn, in a suit of Arthurian armor, and gradually heats up under the mounting sun in what he calls "that stove"; and a fly gets between the bars of his visor; and he cannot reach his handkerchief in his helmet to wipe the sweat from his streaming face; and at last when he cannot bear it any longer, and dismounts at the side of a brook, and makes the distressed damsel who has been riding behind him take off his helmet, and fill it with water, and pour gallon after gallon down the collar of his wrought-iron cutaway, you have a situation of as huge a grotesqueness as any that Cervantes conceived.

The distressed damsel is the Lady Corisande; he calls her Sandy, and he is troubled in mind at riding about the country with her in that way; for he is not only very doubtful that there is nothing in the castle where she says there are certain princesses imprisoned and persecuted by certain giants, but he feels that it is not quite nice: he is engaged to a young lady in East Hartford, and he finds Sandy a fearful bore at first, though in the end he loves and marries her, finding that he hopelessly antedates the East Hartford young lady by thirteen centuries. How he gets into King Arthur's realm, the author concerns himself as little as any of us do with the mechanism of our dreams. In fact, the whole story has the lawless operation of a dream; none of its prodigies are accounted for; they take themselves for granted, and neither explain nor justify themselves. Here he is, that Connecticut man, foreman of one of the shops in Colt's pistol factory, and full to the throat of the invention and the self-satisfaction of the nineteenth century, at the court of the mythic Arthur. He is promptly recognized as a being of extraordinary powers and becomes the king's right-hand man, with the title of The Boss; but as he has apparently no lineage or blazon, he has no social standing, and the meanest noble has precedence of him, just as would happen in England today. The reader may faintly fancy the consequences flowing from this situation, which he will find so vividly fancied for him in the book; but they are simply irreportable. The scheme confesses allegiance to nothing; the incidents, the facts, follow as they will. The Boss cannot rest from introducing the apparatus of our time, and he tries to impart its spirit with a thousand most astonishing effects. He starts a daily paper in Camelot; he torpedoes a holy well; he blows up a party of insolent knights with a dynamite bomb; when he and the king disguise themselves as peasants, in order to learn the real life of the people, and are taken and sold for slaves, and then sent to the gallows for the murder of their master, Launcelot arrives to their rescue with five hundred knights on bicycles. It all ends with the Boss's proclamation of the Republic after Arthur's death, and his destruction of the whole chivalry of England by electricity.

We can give no proper notion of the measureless play of an imagination which has a gigantic jollity in its feats, together with the tenderest sympathy. There are incidents in this wonder-book which wring the heart for what has been of cruelty and wrong in the past, and leave it burning with shame and hate for the conditions which are of like effect in the present. It is one of its magical properties that the fantastic fable of Arthur's far-off time is also too often the sad truth of ours; and the magician who makes us feel in it that we have just begun to know his power, teaches equality and fraternity in every phase of his phantasmagory.

He leaves, to be sure, little of the romance of the olden time, but no one is more alive to the simple, mostly tragic poetry of it; and we do not remember any book which imparts so clear a sense of what was truly heroic in it. With all his scorn of kingcraft, and all his ireful contempt of caste, no one yet has been fairer to the nobility of character which they cost so much, too much to develop. The mainly ridiculous Arthur of Mr. Clemens has his moments of being as fine and high as the Arthur of Lord Tennyson; and the keener light which shows his knights and ladies in their child-like simplicity and their innocent coarseness throws all their best qualities into relief. This book is in its last effect the most matter-of-fact narrative, for it is always true to human nature, the only truth possible, the only truth essential, to fiction. The humor of the conception and of the performance is simply immense; but more than ever Mr. Clemens's humor seems the sunny break of his intense conviction. We must all recognize him here as first of those who laugh, not merely because his fun is unrivalled, but because there is a force of right feeling and clear thinking in it that never got into fun before, except in *The Bigelow Papers*. Throughout, the text in all its circumstances and meaning is supplemented by the illustrations of an artist who has entered into the wrath and the pathos as well as the fun of the thing, and made them his own.

NEWSPAPER ARTICLE By Ernest Hemingway
Kansas City Star - April 21, 1918

"MIX WAR, ART AND DANCING"

Outside a woman walked along the wet street-lamp lit sidewalk through the sleet and snow.

Inside in the Fine Arts Institute on the sixth floor of the Y.W.C.A. Building, 1020 McGee Street, a merry crowd of soldiers from Camp Funston and Fort Leavenworth fox trotted and one-stepped with girls from the Fine Arts School while a sober faced young man pounded out the latest jazz music as he watched the moving figures. In a corner a private in the signal corps was discussing Whistler with a black haired girl who heartily agreed with him. The private had been a member of the art colony at Chicago before the war was declared.

Three men from Funston were wandering arm in arm along the wall looking at the exhibition of paintings by Kansas City artists. The piano player stopped. The dancers clapped and cheered and he swung into "The Long, Long Trail Awinding". An infantry corporal, dancing with a swift moving girl in a red dress, bent his head close to hers and confided something about a girl in Chautauqua, Kas. In the corridor a group of girls surrounded a tow-headed young artilleryman and applauded his imitation of his pal Bill challenging the colonel, who had forgotten the password. The music stopped again and the solemn pianist rose from his stool and walked out into the hall for a drink.

A crowd of men rushed up to the girl in the red dress to plead for the next dance. Outside, the woman walked along the wet, lamp lit sidewalk. It was the first dance for soldiers to be given under the auspices of the War Camp Community Service. Forty girls of the art school, chaperoned by Miss Winifred Sexton, secretary of the school, and Mrs. J. F. Binnie were the hostesses. The idea was formulated by J. P. Robertson of the War Camp Community Service, and announcements were sent to the commandants at Camp Funston and Fort Leavenworth inviting all soldiers on leave. Posters made by the girl students were put up at Leavenworth on the interurb an trains.

The first dance will be followed by others at various clubs and schools throughout the city according to Mr. Robertson.

The pianist took his seat again and the soldiers made a dash for partners. In the intermission, the soldiers drank to the girls in fruit punch. The girl in red, surrounded by a crowd of men in olive drab, seated herself at the piano, the men and the girls gathered around and sang until midnight. The elevator had stopped running, and so the jolly crowd bunched down the six flights of stairs and rushed waiting motor cars. After the last car had gone, the woman walked along the wet sidewalk through the sleet and looked up at the dark windows of the sixth floor.

NEWSPAPER ARTICLE By Ernest Hemingway

Kansas City Star – February 18, 1918

"THRONG AT SMALLPOX CASE"

While the chauffeur and male nurse on the city ambulance, devoted to the carrying of smallpox cases, drove from the General Hospital to the municipal garage on the North Side today to have engine trouble "fixed" a man, his face and hands covered with smallpox pustules, lay in one of the entrances to the Union Station. One hour and fifteen minutes after having been given the call the chauffeur and nurse reported at the hospital with the man, G.T. Brewer, 926 West Forty-second Street. The ambulance had been repaired.

Behind that vehicle was an ambulance from the Emergency Hospital, ordered to get the patient by Dr. James Tyree, in charge of contagious diseases, after repeated calls from the station.

Brewer, a life insurance agent, arrived from Cherryvale, Kas., this morning. At 9 o'clock James McManus, officer in charge of the police station at the depot, found him lying in the west entrance to the lobby. Streams of persons, hurrying past, eddied about Brewer while solicitous passersby asked the trouble. At 9:50 McManus placed a policeman near the sick man to keep persons away.

McManus says he called the contagious department of the hospital immediately after finding Brewer. An ambulance was promised. Two calls were sent to the hospital later and each time, so McManus says, he was told the ambulance was on the way. Doctor Tyree once insisted McManus take the sick man into the police office there, but McManus refused, saying more persons would be exposed. Doctor Tyree also said the ambulance would be there "right away."

When the ambulance did reach the station at 10:15, the driver explained it had been broken down while out on another call.

Doctor Tyree explained later that the regular sick ambulance, No. 90, was wrecked last night. When the call first was received at the receiving ward of the General Hospital at 9:05 o'clock ambulance No. 92, the smallpox carrier, was dispatched, he said.

"But the ambulance had motor trouble," Doctor Tyree continued. "The chauffeur and the male nurse in charge decided to go to the municipal garage and get the trouble fixed."

The garage, on the North Side, is about as far from the hospital as the distance from the hospital to the Union Station and return.

Doctor Tyree criticized the police for failure to remove Brewer to an isolated place instead of leaving him "where scores of travelers came in contact and were exposed to smallpox."

www.edudps.com

WRITE WITH THE BEST – Vol. 1

teaches the following genres:

WRITING A DESCRIPTIVE PARAGRAPH – DESCRIBING AN OBJECT
20,000 Leagues Under the Sea
by Jules Verne

WRITING A DESCRIPTIVE PARAGRAPH – DESCRIBING A PLACE
A Christmas Carol
by Charles Dickens

WRITING A DESCRIPTIVE PARAGRAPH – DESCRIBING A CHARACTER
Robinson Crusoe
by Daniel Defoe

WRITING A DIALOGUE
The Wind in the Willows
by Kenneth Grahame

WRITING A SHORT STORY
"The Gift of the Magi"
by O. Henry

WRITING A FABLE
"The Ants and the Grasshopper"
and
"The Shepherd's Boy and the Wolf"
by Aesop

WRITING A FRIENDLY LETTER
Treasure Island
by Robert Louis Stevenson

WRITING POETRY – RHYMING VERSE
"The Daffodils"
by William Wordsworth

WRITING POETRY – A BALLAD OR NARRATIVE POEM
"Paul Revere's Ride"
by Henry Wadsworth Longfellow

www.edudps.com

OTHER PRODUCTS BY DPS   www.edudps.com

- *WRITE WITH THE BEST* Vol. 1-Grades 3-12 teaches *descriptive* writing skills in nine different genres in an easy to use format • Teaches literary critique, some grammar, proofreading, and listening comprehension skills • Written <u>to</u> the student • Daily lessons in 15-45 minutes • Can be used with other subjects • Has grading criteria for parents and teachers • Contains an answer key • Features a "How-To-Write Guide" for effective writing even after the curriculum is completed • Contains references to additional literary passages for continual use • Has activities for all learning styles/Encourages reluctant writers and accommodates the learning disabled.

- *Roots and Fruits A Comprehensive Vocabulary Curriculum covering Grades K through 12.* This is a thirteen-year curriculum, starting at the kindergarten level. Contains 673 English forms of Greek and Latin roots and prefixes with their meanings, plus 1716 vocabulary words. It increases spelling, writing, dictionary and reading decoding skills. Contains most commonly tested words on the SAT (Scholastic Aptitude Test) as well as words from other standardized tests. Utilizes daily activities and games that appeal to all learning styles. Contains complete lesson plans. Vocabulary for the comprehension of all subjects including world and U.S. history, the sciences, foreign languages, mathematics and geometry, classical literature and reading, and the Bible. Takes as little as 15 minutes a day.

- *The Diagnostic Prescriptive Assessment*-Revised. This is a criterion referenced diagnostic test available in six separate assessments for grades K through 5. Each test is a 4-in-1 tool: (1) a diagnostic test (2) an effective pre-assessment for grade placement (3) provides objectives and scope & sequence for each grade level (4) serves as a yearly evaluation, portfolio, and Individual Educational Plan. • Thoroughly covers all required subjects • High criteria of mastery/Superior Educational Qualifications • No normed standards/True test scores • Grade Level Requirements. It is an excellent preparation tool for times when standardized testing is required. Each test was devised for parents to administer and score (answer key supplied) and comes with a remedial strategies section for correcting academic weaknesses. From 23 to 32 subtests- 51 to 65 pp.

- *The Total Language Diagnostic Assessment with Remedial Strategies and Answer Key*-Revised. This assessment is a compilation of the complete language subtests of *The Diagnostic Prescriptive Assessment*-Revised, K through 5th grades. Its unique features are: (a) A thorough workbook or manual for those who desire to work on language only-covering reading, phonics, reading vocabulary, reading comprehension, spelling, handwriting, composition, and dictionary and English skills. (b) A manual consisting only of actual test items of criterion referenced diagnostic tests. (c) Contains approximately 11 pages of remedial strategies *per grade level* for correcting academic weaknesses discovered through testing. (d) One student can use it for six years of academic requirements. (e) One manual can be used by a family with children ranging from K to 5th grades. It comes in two parts and contains 72 subtests-132 pp.

- *The Concise Learning Styles Assessment with Instructional Guide.* Determines the primary, second, and third level learning preferences, whether visual, auditory, or tactile/kinesthetic-for ages 7 through adult • comes complete with directions for administering and scoring • possesses grading scale for determination of "levels of strength" of each learning style • contains no "fluff" • includes instructional guide with teaching tips for each learning style • helps prevent misdiagnosis of learning problems • helps remove frustration and "burn-out" • can be used by the entire family.

- *The Diagnostic Grade Placement Screening* for grades K through 8. This assessment reveals the functional grade level of your child in reading decoding, math computation, and written expression for proper curriculum placement • Administered and scored by parents (grade key supplied).

- *The Homeschooler's Guide For Learning Problems-Practical Tips For Daily Success* is the only learning problems guide that we know of that has been written specifically for homeschoolers. Other books on the market deal with the student in a regular classroom setting. Our book contains a complete checklist for determining the specific learning problem of the student, as well as giving causes and solutions to the specific problems. It contains no superfluous material and was devised as a result of nineteen years of diagnosing and remediating learning difficulties.

- *The Homeschooler's Guide To Attentional Difficulties-Practical Tips For Daily Success.* Covers subjects such as ADHD-Fact or Fiction? How do I know if it is an attentional problem or another problem? • Takes a non-medication approach to solve attentional problems • Practical modifications to make for your child which will alter his learning experience • Gets right to the issues involved • Contains "Real Life" success stories of homeschooled children • Answers the most frequently asked questions about attentional problems